DEATH, CONTEMPLATION AND SCHOPENHAUER

The connections between death, contemplation and the contemplative life have been a recurrent theme in the canons of both western and eastern philosophical thought. This book examines the classical sources of this philosophical literature, in particular Plato's *Phaedo* and the *Katha Upanishad* and then proceeds to a sustained analysis and critical assessment of the sources and standpoints of a single thinker, Arthur Schopenhauer, whose work comprehensively pursues this problem.

Going beyond the well-examined western influences on Schopenhauer, Singh offers an in-depth account of Schopenhauer's references to eastern thought and a comprehensive examination of his eastern sources, particularly Vedanta and Buddhism. The book traces the pivotal issue of death through the whole range of Schopenhauer's writings uncovering the deeper connotations of his crucial notion of the will-to-live.

An excellent book, clear and concise without academic slang. A book for all those who expect from philosophy more than intellectual acrobatics.

Günter Wohlfart
University of Wuppertaal, Germany

According to Raj Singh, Schopenhauer is a thinker "whose philosophical thought revolves around the pivotal issue of death." In this work, a thoughtful examination of Socrates and the Vedantic tradition provides the background for an extensive treatment of the role of death in Schopenhauer's work and its relation to contemplation and the contemplative life. Professor Singh's work is searching, enlightening and revealing.

David Carr
Emory University, USA

Raj Singh considers all of Schopenhauer's published works, focussing on the connection between death, philosophy and the ideal philosophical life. As the first complex study to qualify Schopenhauer's pessimism with reference to Indian thought, this book is timely in light of the recently awakened debate on Schopenhauer's relation to eastern traditions.

Matthias Kossler
Johannes Gutenberg University Mainz, Germany

ASHGATE NEW CRITICAL THINKING IN PHILOSOPHY

The *Ashgate New Critical Thinking in Philosophy* series brings high quality research monograph publishing into focus for authors, the international library market, and student, academic and research readers. Headed by an international editorial advisory board of acclaimed scholars from across the philosophical spectrum, this monograph series presents cutting-edge research from established as well as exciting new authors in the field. Spanning the breadth of philosophy and related disciplinary and interdisciplinary perspectives *Ashgate New Critical Thinking in Philosophy* takes contemporary philosophical research into new directions and debate.

Death, Contemplation and Schopenhauer

R. RAJ SINGH
Brock University, Canada

ASHGATE

Published by
Ashgate Publishing Limited
Gower House
Croft Road
Aldershot
Hampshire GU11 3HR
England

Ashgate Publishing Company
Suite 420
101 Cherry Street
Burlington, VT 05401-4405
USA

Ashgate website: http://www.ashgate.com

British Library Cataloguing in Publication Data
Singh, Ravindra Raj
   Death, contemplation and Schopenhauer. - (Ashgate new
   critical thinking in philosophy)
   1. Schopenhauer, Arthur, 1788-1860 2. Death
   I. Title
   128.5

Library of Congress Cataloging-in-Publication Data
Singh, Ravindra Raj.
   Death, contemplation and Schopenhauer / Ravindra Raj Singh.
      p. cm. -- (Ashgate new critical thinking in philosophy)
   Includes bibliographical references and index.
   ISBN-13: 978-0-7546-6050-7 (hardcover) 1. Death. 2. Contemplation. 3. Schopenhauer,
Arthur, 1788-1860. I. Title.

   BD444.S52 2007
   193--dc22

2006026855

ISBN-13: 978 0 7546 6050 7

Printed and bound in Great Britain by Antony Rowe Ltd, Chippenham, Wiltshire.

Contents

List of Abbreviations

WWR   The World as Will and Representation

W, I   The World as Will and Representation, Vol. 1

W, II   The World as Will and Representaiton, Vol. II

PP, I   Parerga and Paralipomena, Vol. I.

PP, II   Parega and Paralipomena, Vol. II

H N   Der Handschriftliche Nachlass

FRPSR On the Fourfold Root of the Principle of Sufficient Reason

In memoriam

Harbans Raj Singh

(1918–1979)

Prologue

Death and Contemplation

If philosophy begins, as Aristotle says, from wonder,[1] then things that strike wonder in us must be instigators of philosophical thought. Nothing causes more wonder and awe than death, the disconcerting reality of which assails every reflective mind. It is true that the evasion and dismissal of death are as commonplace as the acknowledgement in thought of death as the "only thing about which there is no uncertainty."[2] Death is never taken as a merely physical event. The why, what, wherefore and aftermath of death causes tremendous perturbation and amazement. Furthermore, it is the root of all existential anxiety (*angst*) that prompts humans to absorb themselves in worldliness as Heidegger explains and it is what makes the will-to-live a natural drive, as Schopenhauer upholds. Death is an issue that is ever unresolved. It is what everyone knows but no one has experienced. The amazing truth of death, its meaning and its implications have been explored not only within philosophy but also religion, literature and social sciences. The issues of death and immortality are the backbone of all major religious traditions. Various speculations concerning the meaning of death and the typical human responses to its indubitable reality are widely outlined in the poetry, fiction and non-fiction of all languages. Death and dying has emerged as a major field of inquiry within the social sciences due to its practical and therapeutic importance.

Death and Philosophy

It has been claimed that no other human field of inquiry and creativity is as closely allied to death as philosophy. Indeed, philosophy was conceived as wedded to death. Thus a pertinent issue at hand for us is the following: what is the connection between a thoughtful recognition of death and the activity of philosophizing? Ever since the word and deed of Socrates proclaimed the bond between death and philosophy, the theme of death has stayed with western philosophy as an essential part of its mandate. Since the nature and scope of philosophy has to be one of the foremost issues for philosophy, with an evolutionary process of its own, it is but natural that the theme of death has been embraced and treated somewhat differently in different epochs and different systems of philosophy. But no period of history has found this theme non-essential and unworthy of thought on the whole. In the eastern philosophies

---

1   Aristotle, *Metaphysics*, 982b.

2   St. Augustine, commentary on Psalm 38:19. Quoted by J. Pieper, *Death and Immortality* (New York: Herder & Herder, 1974), p. 17.

of India, China and Japan the issue of death is widely discussed,[3] and its close ties to philosophizing and contemplative living have been variously traced. In Indian philosophy, the connection between death-contemplation and the contemplative life was elucidated in the Vedic texts and the question of death has always been an important theme in the six systems of Hindu thought as well as in Buddhism and Jainism. Death is widely discussed as one of the important themes of philosophy, both in the East and the West. However, occasionally it has been named as *the* theme of philosophy. Why?

> Death is the real inspiring genius or musagetes of philosophy, and for this reason Socrates defined philosophy as '*thanatos melete*' (rehearsal for death). Indeed without death there would hardly have been any philosophizing (W, II, 463).

This reflective assertion by Arthur Schopenhauer (1778–1860) at the head of his famous essay on death outlines his conviction concerning the bond between death and philosophy. Whereas some will regard it as a radical statement about the task and scope of philosophy, for others, it remains a profound description of the connection between death-contemplation and the urge to philosophize. Philosophy is said to be the rehearsal or practice or preparation (*melete*) for death, and the fact of death as the chief inspiration for philosophy. Death is named as the subject-matter, the impetus and the goal of philosophy. Death is described here as not just one among many concerns and issues of philosophy but as "the" business of philosophy. It is said that philosophy sets itself into motion through its fundamental wonder about human death, and by implication about the nature and destiny of human existence. Thus philosophy begins from and remains preoccupied with death through and through.

Why is a thoughtful consideration of death an impetus to philosophize? Some explanations given and suggested in the traditional and modern philosophical texts are as follows:

(a) As one acknowledges death, one is impelled to contemplate the whole of reality, the entirety of human existence, that is, one is obliged and enabled to take into account a wholistic perspective on things. This wholistic perspective, this overcoming of fragmentary, partial and limited approaches is what is requisite for a philosophical assessment of phenomena.

(b) Since death arouses wonder, thinking about death enhances question-worthiness of matters related to death, namely, human existence, human condition, human destiny. Wonder about death turns life into a riddle or an enigma, to be confronted in philosophical thought.

(c) Death-contemplation inspires a non-materialistic and moderate way of life which voluntarily gives up what the vulgar and the thoughtlessly materialistic people take to be "the life." Thus an authentic philosophical life practices death by choosing "dying" (that is, renouncing) over "living," (that is, common living of excessive worldly pursuits). Thus death-contemplation inspires the

---

3   See F.H. Holck, *Death and Eastern Thought* (New York: Abingdon Press, 1974).

philosopher for a genuinely philosophical living of moderation, simplicity and detachment from the world.

(d) Death-contemplation inspires the thinker to invoke Being of beings, the fundament of all reality. That is why Martin Heidegger (1889–1976) calls death the shrine of Nothing.[4] On the other hand, it inspires a believer to invoke God. It urges a Buddhist to invoke transitoriness and a lack of substantiality (*svabhava*) in all entities. Death inspires a philosophical mind to get to the bottom of its fundamental concepts.

But in asserting all this, are we not overlooking the fact that philosophy has had and continues to have numerous other areas of interest. Whereas inquiry into the existential implications of death continues to be one of the many concerns of philosophy it may not be recognized as its essential task as well as its chief inspiration. As Choron suggests, the place and the role of the problem of death in western philosophical thought may have undergone several transformations in different periods of its history.[5] Choron believes that the absence of "very definite religious convictions in the fifth and fourth century B.C. in Greece (as well as) in second and first century in Rome" accounts for death having been deemed as "a motif and a motive of philosophy." But with the advent of Christianity and its concepts of resurrection and eternal life, philosophy no longer needed to deal with death. Choron acknowledges that the preoccupation with death within theology, poetry and sculpture continued in the Christian era leading to an obsession with death in the fourteenth and fifteenth centuries. With the re-emergence of independent philosophical thought during the Renaissance, a denial of personal immortality became a dominant view of the philosophers of the times and remained a dominant philosophical stance up to the nineteenth century. Choron remarks that the problem of death was reduced to being that of *ars moriendi*, of "mastering the fear of death and preventing it from poisoning the enjoyment of life." Some philosophers, however, never gave up on the pursuit of ever-new proofs of the immortality of the soul.

> On the whole, however, as philosophy becomes an independent discipline, it evolves and concentrates on its own specifically philosophical problems; death as a motif of philosophizing becomes an exception. Thus, in addition to the differences between philosophies as to the kind of answer to death which they provide, there is another difference to be noted: namely, whether they deal with the problem of death or disregard it completely.[6]

Philosophy is supposed to be a "free science" with its nature and scope being the burning issues, never conclusively defined but purposely kept open-ended. There

---

4 Martin Heidegger, "The Thing", trans. A. Hofstadter, in *Poetry, Language, Thought* (New York: Harper & Row, 1971), p. 178.

5 J. Choron, *Death and Western Thought* (New York: Macmillan Company, 1963), pp. 265–73.

6 Ibid., p. 267.

is something beautiful as well as valuable about a philosopher asserting their own well-reasoned view of what philosophy is all about. That there is no absolutely acceptable conception of the nature and the task of philosophy makes it the most pre-suppositionless field of knowledge and in the opinion of some, the most rigorous and sovereign science. While Choron's historical sketch is quite insightful and his conclusions quite realistic, it may be noted that no period of the history of ideas and no tradition of human thought shows a complete disregard of the problem of death. Thus, Pieper shows the same realism in his modification of the Socratean assertion "philosophy, the practice of death" to "death, an especially philosophical subject."[7] Leading thinkers from all eras have responded to the Socratean conviction concerning the intertwining of death and philosophy in the thanatological slants adopted in their own systems. Schopenhauer and Heidegger have certainly incorporated the Socratean insight in their respective systems. In the East, the connection between Being, death and thoughtful living elucidated in the texts such as the *Katha Upanishad*, remains explored, cultivated and retold in numerous later philosophical and religious works.

It is true that death-contemplation can no longer be imposed as a required condition for the authenticity of a philosophical work. However, if the activity of philosophizing is not to be completely detached from the philosophical life and if moral living is to remain a goal of all moral speculation, philosophy and philosophers will continue to trace the implications of the "terrible certainty of death." Thinking about death can appropriately be called death-contemplation, for the word "contemplation" conveys the sense of a thoughtful consideration (meditative probe) as well as a thoughtful living. The Latin root *contemplare* means to gaze attentively, view mentally, to meditate, and so on. The Greek term *theoria* means viewing, meditation, as well as both contemplation and the contemplative life. Thus, death-contemplation should mean not only a thoughtful and philosophical assessment of the implications of death but also a thoughtful life in the shade of death, a practice of the life lessons of death.

The Project of This Book

Numerous elucidations of the meaning of death from the philosophical, religious and literary standpoints are to be found in the western and eastern traditions alike. To produce an anthology of the major philosophical analyses and theories concerning the human destiny of death even within a single tradition is an enormous task. Nevertheless, several such anthologies have been published.[8]

Our study is specifically concerned with an exposition of the problem of the connection between death, contemplation and the contemplative life rather than that of the meaning and implications of death in general. Although these two philosophical enigmas are inter-related, in this book, we will focus on discovering how philosophy and philosophical life can be viewed as involved with death. Such

7   Pieper, *Death and Immortality*, p. 9.
8   For example, Choron, *Death and Western Thought*; Holck, *Death and Eastern Thought*.

issues of fundamental philosophical and existential importance can be studied either through an historical survey of several major philosophical texts on the subject or perhaps through a sustained analysis of the sources and standpoints of a single thinker whose work pursues the problem at hand comprehensively.

Adopting the latter approach, we will study Schopenhauer's philosophical work from the standpoint of the problem of the connection between death, contemplation and contemplative life. Of course, Schopenhauer's entire analytic of the meaning of death and the allied philosophical issues will expose themselves while we pursue our specific problem within his work. At the same time, in the initial chapters of the book, two classical western and eastern philosophical analyses of the problem shall be outlined. These pioneering standpoints of the connection between death and contemplation served as inspirations for philosophy and philosophical living within their respective traditions. Whereas these classical standpoints on death and contemplation expose this all-important philosophical problem in its eastern and western versions, they also happen to be the fundamental sources of Schopenhauer's death-contemplation. Thus this book aims to expose the implicit roots of the explicit sources of Schopenhauer's thought, while pursuing the problem at hand independently as well as within this thinker's system.

In the later chapters of the book, Schopenhauer's standpoints on the connection between death and contemplation (inclusive of contemplative life), in his own terms, that between death and the denial of the will-to-live, shall be thoroughly exposed. An attempt will be made to identify his sources, influences and pre-suppositions through the development of his thought on the subject of thanatology. His readings and interpretations of Indian systems of thought, particularly Vedanta and Buddhism, shall be critically examined.

In Chapter 1, the classic exposition of the problem of death-contemplation attributed to Socrates and as spelled out in Plato's *Phaedo* is outlined. Due emphasis is given to the act of Socrates' philosophical martyrdom and his reported standpoints on the ideal approach to death that a philosopher must have. Although the deed of Socrates is celebrated and well known within western philosophy, to approach it from an existential standpoint, de-emphasizing the proofs of the immortality of the soul and referring to the influence of Socratean thanatology on Plotinus in ancient times and Heidegger in our times, is an original analysis offered by this chapter. The brief portraits of the thanatological achievements of Socrates, Plotinus and Heidegger fully expose the problem at hand in its western format, and set the stage for a fuller discussion of the same problem in Schopenhauer's corpus of work.

In Chapter 2, the problem of death-contemplation in its classic eastern version, quite comparable to its western counterpart, is given. The *Katha Upanishad* tells the tale of the young philosophical mind of Naciketas who encounters Yama, the god of death, in pursuit of philosophical truth. Just as we do so in case of *Phaedo*, we identify the symbolic messages of the text of the *Katha Upanishad* on the issue of the bond between death and philosophy. In the literal expositions of these texts that are available in the secondary literature, these subtle messages of the texts are scarcely noticed, and the existential problem itself lies buried in examples of literal conceptual juggling. The *Katha Upanishad* had a tremendous impact on mainstream Vedanta thought and on various other thanatological thinkers such as Kabir. We will show in later chapters that Schopenhauer, who was well versed in his reading of the Upanishads, was greatly influenced by the central insights of Vedanta. Thus it is vital to expose an eastern classic of thanatology for the purposes of a fuller appreciation of the problem as such and for fully comprehending the ultimate sources of Schopenhauer's thought.

Chapter 3 introduces us to the full flowering of the ancient problem of death-contemplation in Schopenhauer's system through an exposition of the treatment of this problem in Book IV of this thinker's *magnum opus*. This division of *The World as Will and Representation* (*WWR*) presents the problem in forms of the denial of the will-to-live, which we argue, is simply Schopenhauer's way of re-emphasizing the practice of death. Thus physical death and ideal life in the shade of death are creatively intertwined by Schopenhauer in truly Socratean manner, which at the same time employs the insights of Vedanta and Buddhism to present a classic trans-cultural body of philosophical work.

In Chapter 4, the issue of Schopenhauer's eastern influences, particularly Indian philosophies of Vedanta and Buddhism is fully examined. Schopenhauer's readings of Indian concepts widely incorporated into his own system are critically examined while his unique ability to treat world philosophy as one body of knowledge is noted. It may seem to some readers that the issue of Schopenhauer's debt to Vedantic and Buddhist insights and concepts is examined as a general assessment in this chapter. It may be so, but such an appraisal is necessary for the full elucidation of the chief problem of our project, namely, the connection between death and contemplation with special reference to Schopenhauer's thought.

Chapter 5 studies the supplementary materials on the subject-matter of death and contemplation that are to be found in Volume II of *WWR*. Many of these essays of Schopenhauer loosely connected with the chapters of Book IV of Vol. I, have added insights on the problem and show even stronger influences from the eastern sources, consistent with his further studies of eastern texts. Our pointers toward eastern influences are by no means an attempt to de-emphasize this thinker's western sources. We simply wish to complete the picture, which is currently left half done in the secondary literature, which by and large refers only to Schopenhauer's western influences, such as classical Greek and Latin authors, Plato, Kant, and so on.

In Chapter 6, the works other than *WWR*, published in Schopenhauer's lifetime, particularly the popular collection *Parerga and Paralipomena*, are examined to show that Schopenhauer had an abiding interest in the problem of death-contemplation which appears in all phases of his creative life. Whereas this chapter traces the newer insights and newer references made by Schopenhauer in his later works with due attention to both western and eastern sources, we have purposely confined ourselves to the works published in his lifetime. The additional scholarly baggage of his unpublished manuscripts, letters, diaries, and so on, has not been undertaken in this short book, for these materials simply echo what Schopenhauer wished to present to the world.

Chapter 1

The Word and the Deed of Socrates

In the western philosophical tradition, the remarkable life and death of Socrates is, in itself, a classic statement on the bond between death and a contemplative life. That Socrates himself elucidated this connection between a philosophical life and the practice of death in his last conversation with his friends, shortly before his martyrdom, was recorded by Plato in his classical work *Phaedo*. In this chapter, we will trace the details of Socrates' classical statement on death and contemplation, both in his word and in his deed, and, in brief, the impact of his thanatology on the philosophical missions of Plotinus and more recently of Martin Heidegger. The works of these thinkers in the ancient and the contemporary periods of western thought are but twin examples of the spell cast by Socrates on one of the fundamental issues of philosophy and how the message of the father of western philosophy is understood and incorporated by some of the outstanding thinkers of subsequent generations.

The impact of the Socratean thanatological insights on Schopenhauer will be traced in much more detail in the body of this book. However, a brief elucidation of the philosophical problem of death-contemplation and of the classical sources of this issue along with some examples from the history of philosophy will not only offer a clarification of the problem itself, but also of how the same problem is to be traced in Schopenhauer's work. Thus our study offers a look not only at Schopenhauer's sources but the sources of his sources, which happens to be the subject-matter of our next chapter as well. Of course, Heidegger's work cannot be viewed as an influence on Schopenhauer but is being illustrated here for comparative purposes; our account shows that even though Schopenhauer and Heidegger are poles apart on their stance on metaphysics, they are, nevertheless, the heirs to Socratean death-contemplation.

Socrates, The Death-Contemplator

The bond between the contemplative practice of death and being an authentic philosopher was exposed lucidly and dramatically by Socrates, rightly called the martyr of philosophy, who made his final statement on this bond while drinking the hemlock readily and cheerfully.[1] To learn about Socrates' way of living and philosophizing, crowned by his remarkable death, scholars have good reasons to rely

---

1   An earlier version of the first part of this chapter appeared in my article "Death-Contemplation and Contemplative Living: Socrates and the *Katha Upanishad," Asian Philosophy*, 4 (1994): 9–16.

upon Plato's testimony.[2] In reading Plato's *Phaedo* one realizes that the answer to the question concerning death-contemplation and philosophizing is neither obvious nor simple:

> *Simmias:* The many when they hear your words will say … that philosophers are in reality moribund, and that they have found them out to be deserving of the death which they desire…. *Socrates:* And they are right Simmias in thinking so, with the exception of the words "they have found them out," for they have not found out either in what sense the true philosopher is moribund and deserves death, or what manner of death he deserves.[3]

To learn what Socrates maintained concerning death-contemplation, and to reflect upon the motives behind his words, *Phaedo* remains an authentic source. In this work, an account is given not only of Socrates' views, but the goings-on of his death-day are presented in a way that sketches his whole personality. Most analytic philosophical interpretations of this dialogue concentrate on the reported statements of Socrates and ignore what the drama as a whole suggests. When it comes to outlining Socrates' view of death too much attention is given to the various proofs of the immortality of the soul. In fact, these proofs do not constitute the vital content of Socrates' fundamental attitude towards death. Some statements of Socrates suggest that he was hardly convinced of their credibility himself.[4] The major theme of the work, which also constitutes its lasting value, is Socrates' explanations of why death-contemplation must be cultivated by a true philosopher. And this explanation lies not only in his reported words but also in what we know of his exemplary life and death.

In the introductory conversation between Echecrates and Phaedo when the former implores the latter to describe the manner of Socrates' death, the reply includes the remark: "philosophy was the theme of our conversations."[5] The dialogue tells us that Socrates chose to spend his last moments philosophizing with his friends. As death was looming in his as well as in everybody else's mind in this heavy hour, philosophy did not fail to be around. Socrates informed his friends that by being ready to die he was not doing anything strange. "The true votary of philosophy is … of his own accord … always engaged in the pursuit of dying and death."[6] To describe the kind of death the philosopher practices all his life, Socrates speaks about the distinct nature of the body and soul. A true philosopher is said to be concerned about the life of the soul which is obtained at the cost of the death of the body. This death of the body is not achieved either by torturing or annihilating the body but by

---

2   J. Burnet, *Plato's Phaedo* (Oxford: Oxford University Press, 1972), pp. ix–lvl. Burnet maintains that Plato's "opportunities for learning to know Socrates as he really was were vastly greater than those of Xenophon," p. xxix.

3   Plato, *Phaedo*, Benjamin Jowett (trans.), in *Dialogues of Plato* (Chicago, IL: Encyclopaedia Britannica, 1952), 64b [subsequently abbreviated as *Phaedo*].

4   Ibid., 63c.

5   Ibid., 58, 59a.

6   Ibid., 64a.

attaining a freedom from the excessive concern with the body and matters bodily. It is achieved by freeing one's soul from bodily involvement and making it ready for 'pure thought': "Thought is best when the mind is gathered into itself … when it takes leave of the body, and has as little as possible to do with it, when it has no bodily sense or desire, but is aspiring after true being."[7]

A superficial reading of this quotation may lead us to believe that Plato is describing Socrates as an enemy of the body, and as one who really emphasized the separation between the body and the soul. However, this simplistic interpretation withers as we think about Socrates' purpose in positing this distinction. The autobiographical remarks in the dialogue inform us that after his early disappointment with the teachings of Anaxagoras and with the science "that tries to apprehend things by the help of particular senses," Socrates decided to "retreat to the domain of reasoning and seek there the truth of existence."[8] Thus he widened and philosophically defined the Greek conception of the soul (*psyche*) to teach that one could attain neither true knowledge nor virtue by relying upon the bodily senses. The true being of things could only be apprehended by the soul's dwelling in thought, "dwelling in its own place alone, as in another life, so also in this, as far as it can."[9] The phrase "as in another life, so also in this" is significant. It indicates that Socrates believes that as the philosopher practices such a death, the soul sustains itself in a "here" and a "hereafter" in this very life.

The "body" here should be understood in its broader context, as representing the worldly involvements of the human being realized through human senses. It is suggested that for the most part, man's soul is in bondage when it is absorbed in mundane concerns. The task of philosophy is to obtain the release of the soul from the concerns of the sense-world, for it is only in this freedom of thought that a deeper and fundamental (that is, ontological) knowledge can be gained. It is this death of the body, that is, death of one's absorption in worldly concerns, that he prescribes for the philosopher. In this state, the soul dwells "as if in another life" without relinquishing "this" life, and is able to "aspire after the true being" of things. For the philosopher, it is a matter of constant practice to let his soul dwell "as far as it can" from bodily concerns, for it is impossible to dismiss "matters bodily" altogether. Besides its ontological rewards, this practice also enables the philosopher to be ready for death, for he or she has already realized that not-being is no evil. Obviously, Socrates' performance on his deathbed was well rehearsed. (lol)

The simple distinction between the body and the soul was posited by Socrates to impress upon people from all walks of life the ethical and ontological role of philosophy. In Plato's reports, he often seems to choose his words and his analytical methods appropriate to his audience. In *Phaedo*, he is shown as trying to impress upon his friends that the hereafter is in many ways better than this world, and as alluding to the myths of the times. It is not hard to notice that he is doing so primarily

---

7 Ibid., 65c.
8 Ibid., 97d, 99c.
9 Ibid., 67c.

for the sake of his audience. He is basically appealing to the credulity of his friends, whereas his own skepticism and indifference is apparent from remarks such as "I am as certain as I can be of such matters", and "shall I suggest that we speculate a little together about the probabilities of these things?."[10] It is clear that the chief reason for his ready acceptance of death is not that he has found a valid proof of the immortality of the soul. The foremost reason for his cheerful resignation is that he is already adept in the philosophical practice of death, that is, in the practice of the renunciation of the world in thought and in the practice of living thoughtfully.

Plotinus and the Legacy of Socrates

Plotinus is a thinker who pursues the Socratean heritage in many ways, especially on the issue of death contemplation. Porphyry's account informs us that Plotinus' thought showed itself in his frugal living. It was a life devoted to the contemplation of the Real, the One, *to agathon*, the Father of all Being. Porphyry was a witness to the realizations of this thinker, for whom philosophy was neither a study of abstractions, nor a building of systems: "To this godlike man who often raised himself in thought, according to the ways Plato teaches in the *Banquet*, to the first and transcendent god, that god appeared who has neither shape nor intelligible form."[11] Porphyry paints the picture of a man who lived his philosophy. According to him Plotinus "never relaxed his self-turned attention except in sleep; even sleep he reduced by taking very little food ... and by his continuous turning in contemplation to his *nous*."[12]

Plotinus' philosophy is aptly considered as a pioneering work of Neoplatonism, for he is clearly building upon the foundations laid by Plato's metaphysics. The notions of the Good (*to agathon*), *nous* and soul were all exposed systematically at first in Plato's writings. However, Plotinus shows remarkable originality in his orderly description of reality based on the intertwining roles of these three hypostases. But perhaps, such sparks of originality are spontaneous rather than deliberately pursued. As Pierre Hadot remarks, among the writers of late antiquity, not originality but fidelity to a tradition was considered the foremost duty.[13] In our brief outline of Plotinus' thought on the theme of contemplative life, we will illustrate Plotinus' fidelity to Plato's thought with respect to contemplation as such. We will particularly explore how exactly Plotinus exposes and supplements the insight contained in Plato's *Phaedo* concerning the connection between death and contemplation.

As we have noted above, contemplation is viewed as a turning away from the "matters bodily" or thoughtless and excessive worldliness by Plato, who is second to none in his downgrading of the visible and the mundane for the sake of a vision

---

10 Ibid., 63c, 70b.

11 Porphyry's *Life of Plotinus*, in A.H. Armstrong (ed. and trans.), *Plotinus* (New York: Collier Books, 1962), p. 48 [subsequently abbreviated as *Plotinus*].

12 Ibid., p. 46.

13 Pierre Hadot, *Plotinus or the Simplicity of Vision*, Michael Chase (trans.) (Chicago, IL: University of Chicago Press, 1993), p. 17.

of the real and the ideal. In keeping this ideal of contemplation alive in his life and works, Plotinus too shows a longing for the absolute, based upon a "turning away" from excessive worldliness. The Platonic themes of man's bond with the absolute, the pursuit of death-contemplation on the part of the philosopher and contemplative and virtuous living, receive Plotinus' creative attention in the *Enneads*.

In his essay "Plato's Doctrine of Truth,"[14] Heidegger attempts to correct the overly ethical interpretation of *to agathon* implicit in its usual translation as "the Good." According to him, *to agathon* is Plato's concept of Being and must be treated as an ontological notion. It is remarkable that Plotinus understands the One as not only beyond any ethical characterization and beyond the intelligible realm of *nous* but also beyond Being. He calls it "not Being but the generator of Being."[15] He conceives man's bond with this attributeless ultimate as the most vital and most fulfilling of all relations and involvements.

To know the One does not mean being able to describe it. Knowing the One is like thought's constant quest to appropriate something real but elusive. Plotinus remarks in the fifth *Ennead* that "we ought not to apply any terms to It; but we should so to speak run round and outside of it trying to interpret our own feelings about it, sometimes drawing near and sometimes falling away in our perplexities about It."[16] This seems to be an accurate description of the contemplative attitude in which the object of one's meditation is elusive, yet the onward swell of one's devotion brings one to the brink of an experience of a momentary but momentous union, only to lapse into an inevitable but renewed return to the familiar mundaneness. According to Plotinus, man has an instinctual bond with the absolute, but remains for the most part forgetful of it: "Men have forgotten that which from the beginning, now still, they want and long for. For everything reaches out to that and longs for It by necessity of nature, as if divining by instinct that it cannot exist without It."[17]

This contemplative realization was recognized as the best attainment of human life by Plotinus. The human being is hardly human without this experience. It is described as a challenge and a "contest" by Plotinus; a contest in the double sense. It is a contest as a striving for something most valuable as well as a hard-won and rare communion between man's longing and divine grace: "Here the greatest, the ultimate contest is set before our souls; all our toil and trouble is for this, not to be left without a share in the best of visions. The man who attains this is blessed in seeing that blessed sight, and he who fails to attain it has failed utterly."[18] In outlining the conditions requisite for such a contemplative practice, Plotinus seems to rely upon the exposition of contemplation given in Plato's writings.

---

14 Martin Heidegger, "Plato's Doctrine of Truth," John Barlow (trans.), in W. Barrett and H.D. Aiken (eds), *Philosophy in the Twentieth Century* (New York: Random House, 1962), Vol III, pp. 251–70.

15 *Plotinus*, V. 2. 1., p. 51.

16 Ibid., VI. 9. 3., p. 55.

17 Ibid., V. 5, 12, p. 62.

18 Ibid., I. 6. 7, p. 126.

Many comparative studies of Plotinus and Plato, and several translators' notes tracing the roots of Plotinus' allusions to Plato's dialogues concentrate, especially in case of *Phaedo* on the various proofs of the soul's immortality, or refer to those parts where mythological accounts are given of the soul's destiny after death and its journey toward Hades. The chief insight of the dialogue concerning the reason why death-contemplation must be cultivated by a genuine philosopher is only mentioned in passing by such analytical readers of the dialogue. Thus, Socrates' influence on Plotinus is not to be traced merely in Plotinus' literal references to Plato in the *Enneads* but also in his general attitude toward contemplation as such and in what Porphyry tells us about Plotinus' own philosophical life and solitary death.

The dialogue *Phaedo* shows us that a clear choice was made by Socrates to remain engaged in philosophizing with his friends in his very last hours. Socrates is reported to have said that his readiness and willingness to die was not anything strange, given his life as a philosopher: "The true votary of philosophy is … of his own accord … always engaged in the pursuit of dying and death."[19] This "dying and death" is not meant as an actual rejection of the corporeal body but an ongoing attempt to secure freedom from an indulgent service of the body, that is, a freedom from the vulgar and thoughtless materialistic pursuits. What is crucial for the realization of a higher contemplative life is a continuing attempt to free one's soul from "matters bodily" and making it ready for pure thought. It is described in the *Phaedo* that true Being can only be intuited by the soul's dwelling in thought. As the philosopher's life becomes a continual rehearsal of such a death, that is, death of the subservience to the body, the soul experiences the here and the hereafter in this very life. The dwelling in the "other life" is particularly useful for the philosopher for it enables him or her to acquire a critical distance from things he or she is supposed to philosophize about. Thus death-contemplation is bound to deliver, not only a holistic and existential perspective, but also the capacity for a detached outlook. The contemplative life also enables one to be free of the fear of actual death, as Socrates demonstrated, for such a philosopher has already realized that not-being (for the sake of the world) is no evil, but contemplation is human life's highest and most blissful potential.

Plotinus seems to have imbibed this contemplative culture full well in his own life and seems to have taught by example to his disciples, according to Porphyry's reports. To the Socratean call to the true philosopher to dwell, "as far as possible" away from the body, "as if in another life", Plotinus adds: "shut your eyes and change to and wake another way of seeing, which everyone has but few use."[20] If we take the *Enneads* literally, Plotinus has a lot to say about the desirability and rewards of contemplation and about the necessity to downplay the matters bodily. At the same time, when we take into account his life and work on the whole, he appears to be an excellent practitioner and expositor of the kind of death-contemplation outlined by Socrates.

---

19 *Phaedo*, 64 a.
20 *Plotinus*, I. 6. 7–8, p. 127.

In what is believed to be his last treatise, Plotinus meditates on death and in the Socratean fashion offers a summary of his entire philosophy. This is why Porphyry placed it in the first *Ennead*. St. Ambrose translates and quotes it in his sermon *De bono mortis*:

> If life and the soul exist after death, then death is good, all the more so in that the soul is better able to carry out her proper activities without the body … In general … there is no evil for the soul who has maintained her purity; and if she has not maintained it then it is not death that is an evil for her but rather life.
>
> It could perhaps be said that, in and of itself, life within the body is an evil but that thanks to virtue, the soul can come to be within the Good, not by living the life of the composite (of soul and the body) but by separating herself from it already in this life.[21]

That the contemplative life does not demand a ruthless suppression of the body is but a practice of detachment of the soul from excessive mundaneness is obviously maintained in Plotinus' standpoint. The abovementioned statement seems to endorse what Socrates is reported to have said to his friends just before his death. The death that the contemplative life undergoes is a death of excessive bodily involvements, a practice of virtue whereby the soul attempts to achieve a separation, as far as possible from the body in this very life. Plotinus seems to allude to the Socratean notion of the desirability of a rehearsal for death in the fourth treatise of the first *Ennead*:

> The common life of body and soul cannot possibly be the life of well being. Plato was right in maintaining that the man who intends to be wise and happy … must look to that Good and be made like it and live by it … .
>
> He must give to this bodily life as much as it needs and he can, but he is himself other than it and free to abandon it, and he will abandon it in nature's good time, and always plans for it with independent authority.[22]

According to Plotinus the world of sense itself is not to be disparaged or dismissed. It mirrors the absolute and represents its mystery:

> Will anyone be so sluggish in mind and so immovable that when he sees all the beauties of the world of sense all its proportion and mighty excellence of its order, and its splendour of form which the stars for all their remoteness make manifest, he will not be seized with reverence and think "what wonders and from what a source?" If he does not, he neither understands the world of sense nor sees that higher world [23]

The world of sense and the higher world are not mutually exclusive and the outright dismissal of the visible reality is not desired. Plotinus' thought is imbued with love and blissful enjoyment of all that is in Being. At the same time, he seems to understand the reasons for Plato's body-soul dualism. Plotinus is fascinated by the Platonic dismissal of the body but realizes that the body stands not for the human physique

---

21 Hadot, *Plotinus or the Simplicity of Vision*, pp. 107, 108.
22 *Plotinus*, I. 4. 16, pp. 132–3.
23 Ibid., II. 9. 16, p. 134.

as such but for "matters bodily" or human being's thoughtless and matter-of-course involvements in mundane projects. The rewards of contemplation do not end with the ending of the meditative moment of union with the One but the contemplator returns to the worldly life with a new resoluteness and renewed inclination toward the contemplative life:

> When a man falls from the vision, he wakes again the virtue in himself in all his order and beauty, and is lightened and rises through virtue to *nous* and through wisdom to the divine. This is the life of gods and divine and blessed men, deliverance from the things of this world, a life which takes no delight in the things of this world, escapes in solitude to the solitary.[24]

The contemplative life is based on a "turning away" from the things of this world or the common worldly concerns which flood the mind and impede its progress through wisdom to the divine. Such a turning away in thought is not an outright dismissal or denial of the visible world but a life of beauty, virtue and moderation. It is an invitation to death to abide in the midst of and alongside life. In outlining his concept of contemplation, Plotinus certainly responds to the insight concerning the practice of death spelled out in *Phaedo*. He seems to demonstrate and supplement the Platonic notion of death-contemplation in an original way in his life and work.

Heidegger as an Heir to Socrates

In the long line of death-contemplators in western philosophy, the contemporary German philosopher Martin Heidegger occupies an illustrious position. Heidegger refers to Socrates and Plato as part of his critique of the history of western metaphysics. One of the questions he raises is whether we should regard Socrates as a pre-metaphysical and a pre-Platonic thinker? Heidegger's work shows an actualization of Socrates' insight about the essential bond between death-contemplation and philosophy. Heidegger can be named a true heir to Socrates because he acknowledges and incorporates the bond between death-contemplation and thinking in his chief work, *Being and Time*, as well as in his later works. The consideration of death is not confined to the initial sections 43–53 of Division II, which deal with Dasein's Being-toward-death explicitly, but is taken up again and again throughout the remainder of this division. Heidegger considers death-contemplation or anticipation (*Vorlaufen*) of death as inseparable from authenticity (*Eigentlichkeit*), resoluteness (*Entschlossenheit*) and temporality (*Zeitlichkeit*) in general.

In his later works, Heidegger drops the term "Dasein" and prefers to call human beings "mortals." Death is called the "shrine of Being" in the essay on "The Thing" and in several of his later essays, the "worlding" of the world is explained in terms

---

24 Ibid., VII. 9. 11, p. 148.

of a gathering of the fourfold (*Geviert*) of earth and sky, the divine and the mortals.[25] Mortality is given its due fundamental status in the emergence of all worldly reality. James M. Demske[26] is misled by his radical assumption when he attempts to contrast Heidegger's position on Death with that of Socrates in the very beginning of his book *Being, Man and Death: A Key to Heidegger*. Heidegger's work calls for a reinterpretation of the *Phaedo*, a matter thoroughly deliberated upon by Henry G. Wolz in his book *Plato and Heidegger*.[27] Among other things, Wolz reflects on human authenticity and "death as a possibility," the two important concepts of Heidegger as very much comparable to the content of the dialogue *Phaedo*. In the conclusion of his very thorough analysis of *Phaedo* from the Heideggerian perspective, Wolz remarks:

> This authenticity as a possibility, according to Heidegger, is offered by the awareness of death which calls the individual from the "they-self" to his true self. Just as uncertainty permeates every aspect of the dialogue, so death as a possibility is present from the first to the last line ... It should now be evident how wrong-headed are the approaches of those who debate over whether or not the arguments logically establish the immortality of the soul ... Nor do those fare better who would simply disregard the arguments as antiquated and concentrate on the dramatic and poetic aspect of the dialogue. For all these are subservient to one single insight: the nature of an authentic commitment in the uncertain atmosphere of the human condition. Such commitment presupposes genuine selfhood which, as Heidegger has shown, is brought out most vividly before us in the face of immanent death.[28]

In his use of the simple concept of the body, Socrates implies that a contemplative person has as little as possible to do with matters bodily, or excessive and thoughtless worldliness. In a comparable manner, Heidegger's focus on authenticity in *Being and Time*, names the thoughtless and matter-of-course existence of Dasein as lostness in the they-self. Both Socrates and Heidegger agree that death-contemplation brings one back to one's real self, called "authenticity" or "ownness" (*Eigentlichkeit*) by Heidegger and "life of the soul" by Socrates.

Socrates' way of thinking is held in special esteem by Heidegger, as he remarks in his *What is Called Thinking*:

> To be capable (of thinking) we must before all else incline toward what addresses itself to thought ... This most thought provoking thing turns away from us ... Once we are ... drawn

---

25 For a relatively more detailed treatment of why Heidegger can be viewed as a Socratic practitioner of death-contemplation, see my article, "Death-Contemplation and Philosophy: Heidegger and the Legacy of Socrates,." *De Philosophia*, 6 (1986): 41–61.

26 James M. Demske, *Being, Man and Death: A Key to Heidegger* (Lexington: University Press of Kentucky, 1970).

27 Henry G. Wolz, *Plato and Heidegger* (London: Associated University Presses, 1981).

28 Ibid., p. 118.

to what withdraws, we are drawing into what withdraws ... whenever man is properly drawing that way, he is thinking ... All through his life and right into his death Socrates did nothing else than place himself into this draft, this current, and maintain himself in it. This is why he is the purest thinker of the west. This is why he wrote nothing.[29]

Heidegger calls all great philosophers after Socrates "fugitives" from this draft, for they let themselves be metaphysicians and system-builders. Socrates, however, through his relentless practice of death, became an adept thinker, who never sacrificed "questions of thinking" for the sake of "answers of metaphysics." Nor did he sacrifice the "living of philosophy" to the "writing of philosophy." Heidegger's homage to Socrates seems to recognize all this.

A Note on the Socratean Dictum and Western Thought

The Socratean insight on the connection between death and philosophy has had a lasting impact on the body of western thought. This impact has been deep-rooted and comprehensive in several ways. First, it is not merely the final discourse of Socrates reported by Plato in his classic *Phaedo* that impressed and intrigued the finest minds of antiquity, such as Aristotle, Seneca, Epictetus, Marcus Aurelius, Plotinus and St. Augustine, but it is also the deed of Socrates and its implications for thought that they found to be truly stunning. *Phaedo* is a drama par excellence, its dramatis personae being no other than life, thought and death. Socrates' insight on death and contemplative life gives an essential assignment to philosophy: to teach men how to die, that is, how to live in the shade of death.

Among the philosophers who have had something or the other to say on the subjects of death, mortal existence, immortality or the hereafter, there have been a distinguished few who have examined the very connection between death and philosophy. It is their belief that death is not only a theme but *the* theme of philosophy and that the very impetus to philosophize issues from a reflection on death. Thus, a distinction is to be made between thinkers who treat death as one of the many themes of philosophy and those who realize and show in their work the conviction that genuine philosophical thinking cannot be done without recognizing death as a central issue in the being of the human entity. Many thinkers in this class have accorded the issue of death a pivotal role in their own systems of thought. In recent times, in their distinct thought-systems, Schopenhauer and Heidegger certainly show their debt to the Socratean dictum. For death certainly is something without which neither the wholeness of Dasein, nor the essence of will-to-live can be conceived. Whereas a comprehensive consideration of death and contemplation (thinking) in Heidegger's thought should be the subject of another book-length study, the later portions of this book will attempt to explore the theme of death and philosophy in Schopenhauer's work. Studying the work of a philosopher who upholds the

---

29 Martin Heidegger, *What is Called Thinking*, J. Glenn Gray (trans.) (New York: Harper and Row, 1968), p. 17.

importance of death-contemplation in his thought should be a well-founded way of considering the problem of the connection between death and philosophy. Such a thematic study must reveal the implicit standpoint of this philosopher on this bond, besides outlining what he explicitly maintains concerning death in his works. We have chosen Schopenhauer's work for a comprehensive study of this nature, which will demonstrate this thinker's response to the call of Socrates, which unmistakably forms the core of his philosophical mission.

In calling death "an especially philosophical subject," Josef Pieper seems to spell out our problem at hand as follows:

> There is absolutely nothing between heaven and earth that cannot set us to philosophizing, that is to say considering the whole of the universe and the whole of existence ... Nevertheless there are subjects which must be called "philosophical" in a stronger sense – because it is in their very nature to compel us to consider the whole of existence. Among these specifically philosophical subjects, that of "death" holds an incomparable place.[30]

The wonder about death is a fundamental wonder that anchors a thinker's gaze toward the grounds of reality. The issue of existence as such looms before one's mind with an urgency demanding answers and resolutions – metaphysical, philosophical, or thoughtful as the case may be. Contemplation is set into motion as one acknowledges death. In the present study, we do not wish to compile numerous historical accolades to and treatments of Socrates' word and deed as outlined in the pages of Plato. Furthermore, our project does not aim at producing another anthology of prominent philosophers' treatments of death. We wish rather to rigorously elucidate the problem of the bond between death and contemplation by way of examining some classic east-west philosophical treatments of the issue. Our outline of these classic expositions and resolutions of the issue will prepare the ground for a comprehensive study, in the later chapters of the book, of the same problem in Schopenhauer's thought. In the next chapter we move from Socrates to the philosophically fertile age of the Vedas in the east, to examine yet another classic of death-contemplation.

---

30 Josef Pieper, *Death and Immortality*, Richard Winston and Clara Winston (trans.) (New York: Herder and Herder, 1974), p. 9.

Chapter 2

The *Katha Upanishad*: An Eastern Classic on Death

The reality of death is of course widely discussed in leading religious and philosophical traditions of the East. The certainty of death and some creatively exposed meanings of death are inevitably pressed into service to confirm the validity of various religious beliefs, dogmas, concepts and systems. This is equally true of the premier eastern philosophical systems which are intertwined with some of the foremost and original religious world-views originating from the morning lands. Thus Hindu, Buddhist, Jain, Confucian, Taoist and Zen thought systems offer a myriad of accounts of the meaning and significance of death. The fact that life and death are placed on a wider canvas of reincarnation and rebirth by Hinduism, Buddhism and Jainism gives a distinctive character and brings additional riddles to the issue of death in eastern thought. Interesting as they might be, detailed accounts of the respective standpoints of various eastern systems on all aspects of human death are beyond the scope of this book. All we can aspire to accomplish in this study is to elucidate some classic standpoints on the relation between death and contemplation, in order to learn more about this relation. In the later chapters of the book, we will trace the bond between death, contemplation and contemplative life in the philosophy of Schopenhauer, which combines splendidly the western and eastern world-views.

As we have seen in the previous chapter, Socrates was a pioneer among the expositors of death and contemplation in the West. His groundbreaking statement in word and deed on death has been esteemed, explored and adopted by numerous subsequent thinkers of the west. This gives an additional meaning to Whitehead's declaration that western philosophy is composed of a series of footnotes to Plato. The existential merit and authenticity of death-realization is widely traced in various Hindu systems of thought. The *Katha Upanishad* is one of the jewels of Vedic literature, known for its succinct description of and for its original response to human wonder about death. This commentary on the role of the contemplation of death in carving out a thoughtful and fulfilled life not only spells out the question concerning death but also provides us with a succinct outline of the fundamentals of the Vedic world-view, systematically presented in the systems of Vedanta philosophy. This *Upanishad* emphasizes that a living of death achieved through relentless practice at turning away from external sense-objects to internal thought-objects blesses one with an immortality in the here and now, which is but the best gift of philosophy. The bond between death and philosophy is fully exposed in the *Katha Upanishad*.

Upanishads are the treatises appended to the Vedas, the oldest texts of the Hindu civilization. *Upanishads* often contain philosophical dialogues alongside mythological, ritualistic and mystical compositions. It is the philosophical content of major *Upanishads* which was systematized for doctrinal purposes by the commentators such as Sankara (eighth century.), Ramanuja (eleventh century) and Madhava (thirteenth century) to propound their own versions of Vedanta philosophy. The *Katha Upanishad* is a short but lucid dialogue that revolves around the issue of death and contemplative life. This celebrated *Upanishad* was commented upon by several reputed expositors of the Vedanta tradition, including Sankara and Ramanuja.

Naciketas, the Philosopher

In this *Upanishad* the story is told of Naciketas, a young aspirant of *vidya* (fundamental knowledge) who goes all the way to the house of death to seek wisdom. The legend of Naciketas, which was also mentioned in the ancient Sanskrit texts such as the *Rig Veda*,[1] *Taittiriya Brahmana*[2] and the epic *Mahabharatha*,[3] refers to an altercation between the youth and his father Vajasravasa. Reacting to his father's donation of some old and milkless cows to the priests as part of the *visvajit* sacrifice ceremony in which one is supposed to give up all one's possessions, Naciketas proposes that he, the son, may also be offered in sacrifice. Assailed by his son's criticism, Vajasravasa angrily says "to death do I give you." Taking his father's word seriously and literally, Naciketas travels to the house of Yama, the sun-god of death, the registrar of the deeds (*karma*) of mortals. Upon arrival, he does not find Yama at home and waits for three nights for his return. When Yama comes back he finds that his servants had neglected to offer due hospitality to a *brahmin* guest (one belonging to the highest caste of the priests). Yama apologizes to Naciketas and offers three boons in lieu of each of the nights he had remained unfed and indifferently treated in his abode. As the first boon, Naciketas asks that upon his return to his father's house, his father may become anxiety-free and may harbour no anger toward him. The second boon asks for instructions concerning the fire-ceremony that could lead mortals to heaven. Both these boons are readily and generously granted by Death, as Naciketas spells out his last request:

> This doubt that there is in regard to a man deceased
> "He exists" say some; "he exists not" say others –
> This would I know, instructed by thee!
> Of the boons this is boon the third.[4]

1   *Rig Veda*, X. 135. See S. Radhakrishnan, *The Principle Upanishads* (London: George Allen and Unwin, 1978), p. 593 (subsequently, *RK*).

2   *Taittiriya Brahmana*, III. 1. 8; *RK*, p. 593.

3   *Mahabharatha, Anusasana Parva*: 106; *RK*, p. 593.

4   *Katha Upanishad*, Robert Ernest Hume (trans.), in *The Thirteen Principle Upanishads* (Oxford: Oxford University Press, 1931), pp. 341–65, 1–20. Hume's translation with minor revisions will be used in long quotations. In short quotations, the translation is often my own. Subsequently, *KU*.

Here begins a dialogue between the young philosopher Naciketas and Yama which is a classic account of the connection between death, contemplation and contemplative life. The *Upanishad* paints a pen-portrait of a true philosopher in the person of Naciketas. The name Naciketas means the "not knower," in Socratean terms, the one who knows that he knows nothing. His father's name Vajasravasa means, as Sankara explains, "one whose fame is consequent on the giving of food."[5] Naciketas lives up to his own and his father's name. The names are obviously well-chosen by the author of the *Upanishad*. Naciketas is adept in the practice of death, the practice of giving up what people call "the good life." He does not fall for the tempting rewards offered by Yama and does not give up the quest for knowledge. He was ready to seek philosophy all the way to the very house of death. Death is clearly shown in the *Upanishad* as the teacher, one that inspires us to explore the meaning of human existence. Death is the true guru whose instruction Naciketas seeks; it is the guru of all true philosophers. The *Upanishad* reveals the gentle face of death. Death is the kind host of philosophers; it offers boons of knowledge to philosophers. To seek wisdom, the philosopher must practice death of the so-called "good life." He or she practises giving up that to which others cling in thoughtless urges. True philosopher is one who lives such a death in order to know. Accordingly, Naciketas says to Yama: "Another teacher of it, like of thee is not to be obtained. No other boon equal of it is there at all."[6] These remarks indicate that for mortals, death is a great teacher. Its lessons are the core of all wisdom.

The third boon sought by Naciketas evokes surprise from Yama who implores the youth to give up this inquiry and offers him long life, sons, grandsons, gold, lands to rule over, damsels and chariots, if he does so. Naciketas says no to these ephemeral things. Who in their right mind would want these things after having been to Yama's abode. "Thine be the vehicles, thine be the dance and song,"[7] says Naciketas, and insists to learn about death from the god of death:

> This thing whereon they doubt, O Death:
> What there is in the great passing-on – tell us that!
> This boon that has entered into the hidden –
> No other than that does Naciketas choose.[8]

As one whose detachment from the worldly and attachment to the philosophical is testified by his rejection of the temptations offered by Yama, Naciketas' main concern is with the issue that has "entered into the hidden" (*gudham anupravista*), that is, a deep philosophical question that provokes philosophical inquiry into other related issues. Naciketas wishes to learn about this "great passing-on" (*samparaye mahati*), about which doubts are usually expressed. The word "great" (*mahati*) is

---

5 Gambhirananda, Swami (ed.), *Eight Upanisads: With the commentary of Sankaracharya* (Calcutta: Advaita Ashrama, 1989), Vol. I, p. 102. Subsequently, *SB*.

6 *KU*, I-22.

7 *KU*, I-26.

8 *KU*, I-29.

used in the sense of being all important. This all-important question concerning passing-on leads naturally to others such as "what is the nature of eternal reality? What is man's relation to it? How can he reach it?", as explained by Radhakrishnan.[9] Sankara remarks in his commentary that the great is the purpose that knowledge concerning the passing-on can serve and identifies this knowledge as the science of soul-assessment (*atmano nirnayno vijnana*). In other words, as thoughtfully pointed out by Sankara,[10] Naciketas is in fact seeking knowledge about the mystery of the Self, a subject deep and hard to contemplate (*gudha gehan durvivechniya*). This interpretation is authenticated by the fact that it is the very mystery of the Self more than anything else that Yama's subsequent discourse seeks to resolve in his comprehensive response to Naciketas. We cannot fail to notice that the *Upanishad* regards death-contemplation as an all-important but enigmatic issue that is intimately connected with the knowledge of the Self, that is, a self-realization in this very life. The key word *samparaye* ("the world beyond") signifies more than its literal meaning. It also refers to passing-on from the life of *maya* ("illusory worldliness") to a contemplative life led in the light of self-knowledge, that is, life of a true philosopher as Socrates outlines in the *Phaedo*.

If we take Naciketas' request literally as inquiring about the "great passing-on," we are perplexed with Yama's answer. Yama for the most part outlines what authentic and inauthentic existence in "this" world is like, rather than painting a portrait of the hereafter. In Yama's instruction to Naciketas, there is nothing comparable to Milton's descriptions of hell in *Paradise Lost* or Dante's details of Inferno, Purgatorio and Paradise in *Divina Commedia*. Yama for the most part expounds on the *atman-jnana* ("soul-knowledge") and its relevance to authentic human existence in "this life." There are some minimal references to karma and rebirth, but their clear-cut assertions do not appear before the fifth chapter (*valli*).

Yama's immediate response in the second chapter concerns human being's ideal existence on this earth. He traces the distinction between good and the pleasant (*sreyas* and *preyas*) and the respective attitudes of the restrained and the thoughtless (*dhira* and *manda*). Presently he declares that wide apart and leading to different ends are *vidya* ("knowledge") and *avidya* ("non-knowledge").[11] *Vidya* is not available to those who "fancy themselves as wise."[12] This passing-on is not apparent to the childish, those who think "this is the only world, there is no other," that is, those totally absorbed in this-worldliness.[13] Sankara in his comment on the passage II.6 refers to two senses of the term *samparaye*: (1) that toward which one goes after death (*sampareyta iti samparayah*), or the world beyond, and (2) the specific means (*sadhana visesa*) revealed by scriptures for the attainment of the world beyond. Thus whereas *samparaye* literally means "the hereafter" as such, it can also mean "passing-

---

9   *RK*, p. 607.
10 *SB*, p. 130.
11 *KU*, II-4.
12 *KU*, II-5.
13 *KU*, II-6.

on" from *avidya* to *vidya*. This latter passing-on is unavailable to the childish and thoughtless (*avivekin*).[14]

Yama further states that this thought is not attained by reasoning (*tarka*) alone. Only a guru who lives it can teach it to a student who deserves it.[15] Yama initiates this teaching by asking the accomplished student Naciketas whether he sees a reality "apart from *dharma* and *adharma* (the moral and the immoral), apart from what is done and not done, apart from what has been and what shall be."[16] Is not Yama inquiring whether Naciketas is aware of the other-worldliness abiding in this worldliness? That Being "desiring which they live the life of brahma-conduct (*brahmacharyam caranti*)" is denoted by the word *aum*:[17]

> This knowing self is not born, nor does it die
> It has not come into being from anything
> Nor anything came into being from it
> This unborn, eternal abiding and primeval
> Is not slain when the body is slain.[18]

"One who is without active will (*akratu*) beholds the Self."[19] Sankara comments that the knower of this *atman* is the "desireless and unstriving one (*akratu*), whose *buddhi* (mind) has been withdrawn from all outer objects, seen or unseen."[20] We may interpret it as follows: the practitioner of death-contemplation realizes the death of visible entities, as well as their invisible meanings and involvements; he or she realizes the death of the visible world and invisible worldliness. The ideas of good conduct, living practice, personal accomplishment, and worthiness of the knower of *atman* (*atman-jnani*), are time and again stressed by Yama:

> This *atman* cannot be obtained by scriptural studies
> Nor by intellect, nor by much learning
> It is obtained by one whom it chooses …
> Not he who has not ceased from bad conduct
> Not the unrestrained, not the unmeditative
> Not one with unpacified mind
> Can attain it by knowledge [*prajna*].[21]

One who cares for *atman* is inclined towards an other-worldliness and lives accordingly, not desiring this worldliness and is unlike the one for whom "this is the only world, there is no other." He practices death for a higher and blissful life,

---

14 *SB*, p. 130.
15 *KU*, II 9.
16 *KU*, II-14.
17 *KU*, II-15.
18 *KU*, II-18.
19 *KU*, II-20.
20 *SB*, 154.
21 *KU*, II-23, 24.

achieves *samparaye* in the here and now. He or she is not an aggressive seeker. He or she waits for *atman* to reveal itself and only practices to be ready for and worthy of its illumination. The bond between the "practice of death" and the "attainments of thought" is indeed precisely revealed by the *Katha Upanishad*:

> Arise ye! Awake ye!
> Obtain your boons and understand them
> A sharpened edge of a razor, hard to traverse
> A difficult path is this – poets declare.[22]

The *Upanishad* urges human beings to arise from their sleep of worldliness and obtain the boons of contemplative life. The boons can be taken as the ultimate contemplative blessings of human life, although Sankara interprets them more narrowly as "approaching the adorable ones, the excellent teachers who know that [Self]."[23] To walk the path of self-knowledge is like walking on the sharp edge of a razor, as declared by the ancient poets. The razor-sharp intellect needed for the ultimate blessing of contemplation is not easily obtained. As described above,[24] only the pure, the restrained, the meditative and one with a pacified mind can traverse on this difficult path. Furthermore, the path is also difficult because a mere meeting of the prerequisites is no guarantee of success. The contemplator may not obtain the touch of the deathless. For the *atman* reveals itself only to one "it" chooses. There is no sure success. The element of grace indicates the loftiness of reward. In other words, this knowledge "arises" in one; it is not "obtained" by one, by the application of a calculative plan.

The life of thoughtless worldliness is called "the net of widespread death" by the *Upanishad* and the pleasure-seekers are called childish:

> The childish go after outward pleasures
> They walk into the net of widespread death
> But the wise knowing immortality
> Seek not the stable among things that are unstable here.[25]

Death-contemplation then is an escape from the widespread death. Only a renunciation of the pursuit of unstable things, a voluntary dying of what the childish call "the good life" brings one in touch with immortality in the here and now. In his commentary on this passage, Sankara remarks:

> Those whose vision of the Self is obstructed by ignorance and thirst, those men of little intelligence, follow only the external desirable things. Because of that reason they get entangled in the snares – those by which one is bound in all pervasive net of association

---

22 *KU*, III-15.
23 *SB*, p. 175.
24 *KU*, II-23, 24.
25 *KU*, IV-2.

with and dissociation from the body-sense-mind complex ... Wise men (*dhirah*) who know *Brahman* would not pray for transient things of the world. For they become aware of immortality – the immortality that they know to be unlike the fake immortality of gods – the immortality that one attains when one gets established in one's Being ... Having known this immortality that is stable and unmoving and which neither increases nor diminishes by *karma*, the knowers of Brahman do not pray for things in this world, for these things cover up the sight of the soul.[26]

The *Upanishad* certainly acknowledges that the wise know an immortality in the here and now, a stability in midst of the enticing and transient things of the world. This contemplative state of soul-assessment can be achieved by voluntarily dying, that is, by voluntarily giving up the so-called "good and high life." This contemplative life amounts to rising above the desire-action complex (*kamakarmasamudaya*) as the intellect is made razor sharp and ready for the matters of the soul.

The Enigma of Reincarnation

The *Upanishad*, besides dwelling on the nature of the universal soul (*brahman*) and the individual soul (*atman*), also expresses the deep-seated conviction of the Vedic tradition concerning reincarnation, a belief that remains intact in other religious traditions of India, namely, Buddhism, Jainism and Sikhism. That the eastern peoples believe in reincarnation is well known. But the religious, philosophical and ontological reasons behind this pervasive belief are hardly ever appreciated. Apparently this predominant myth goes hand in hand with the unity of *Brahman* underneath the diversity of *maya* and *samsara*, in the case of Vedic thought. It is a belief consistent with the explanation of ever-unfolding reality by the theory of dependent origination (*pratitya sumputpada*) in Buddhism. The question whether this belief is to be taken literally or as embodiment of higher philosophical truths by a thoughtful individual is very hard to settle. But the *Katha Upanishad* does indicate toward the deep connection between the realization of the unity of Being (*Brahman*) in contrast with non-knowledge (*avidya*), leading to excessive attachment and clinging to worldliness (*samsara*), resulting in having to be born, and having to die again and again. In a nutshell, we can say that the myth subserves the single most important insight of Vedanta, namely, that an invisible but most real *Brahman* (spirit) pervades everything.

Thus, the tradition literally believes that the *samsara* to which one clings as a matter of course is the *samsara* to which one returns as a matter of course after death. One is bound to it from destiny (based on *karma*) that one has been craving for thoughtlessly. Unless a life of contemplation (*jnana*) transports one to the highway to salvation (*moksha*), *samsara* will remain all in all. Only absolute deliverance (*moksha*) from *samsara* and absolute merger with *Brahman* could be the ultimate consummation of the soul, says Sankara. But the failure to realize the unity of all

---

26 *SB*, p. 183. translation revised.

that is, and remaining caught up in the fascinating and enticing manifold of *samsara* causes reincarnation says the *Katha Upanishad*, quite explicitly:

> Whatever is here, that is there.
> What is there, that again is here.
> He obtains death after death
> Who seems to see a difference here.[27]

The same entity (or human body), which superficially seems to have worldly attributes, here, is in truth rooted in its own reality (*brahman*) which is devoid of worldly attributes. And yet that which is there (*brahman*) established in itself, that very (spirit) appears in diversity, in bodies, in entities of this world. One who is caught up in the diverse reality (that is, takes *maya* as real) and fails to realize the universal spirit, the unity underneath the diversity, is bound to be born again and again and die again and again in *samsara*. Thus one who is attached to *maya* and *samsara* and takes *samsara* as real, is destined to get *samsara* alone as his or her destiny. Such worldlings are left out of the bliss of the spirit (*Brahman*) and remain far away from salvation (*moksha*). Thus one should realize, says Sankara, "I am indeed [*Brahman*] which is homogeneous consciousness and which pervades everything through and through like space."[28]

The *Upanishad* explains next as to how this *Brahman* realization takes place. Obviously, one does not see the unity underneath diversity merely by looking at things while remaining subservient to worldly reality:

> By the mind indeed is this [realization] to be attained
> There is no diversity here at all
> He goes from death to death
> Who seems to see diversity here[29]

Through the mind, this attainment (that is, removal of ignorance (*avidya*)) takes place, explains Sanskara, as one realizes *Brahman* is identical with *atman*, and nothing else (truly) exists.[30] Those who continue to see nothing but diversity remain caught up in the cycle of repeated births and repeated deaths. While the lack of realization of *Brahman* as the Being of all entities is asserted as the cause of the individual soul's reincarnation, it is also discernible that the myth of reincarnation plays a vital role in establishing the Vedic doctrine of *brahman* and *atman*. The belief also serves as a vehicle to impart a subtle intellectual message in a popular form to people in all classes, priests and farmers, city folk and villagers, Sanskrit scholars and illiterate masses alike. The myth creatively imparts the message that all is *brahman* and there is kinship among all entities by asserting that one entity can come back as another

---

27 *KU*, IV-10.
28 *SB*, p. 191.
29 *KU*, IV-11.
30 *SB*, p. 192.

after its superficial annihilation. The bond among all living things is especially recognized in the belief that the soul goes through eighty-four hundred thousand rebirths in as many forms of living beings, before being born as a human entity. The number eighty-four hundred thousand is not a scientific count of all living entities, but a symbolic expression of a vast variety within the totality of living beings on this earth. Just as in the Hindu tradition the myth of reincarnation brings home the message of Brahman abiding in all living beings and in all entities, in Buddhism too the belief in rebirth subserves the all-important doctrine of dependent origination and recognition of a fundamental causality. In Buddhism, rebirth is explained without reference to the so-called soul, on the basis of five attachment groups (*skandhas*) of which the human entity is composed. We will have more occasions to examine the Buddhist doctrine of rebirth in the later chapters of this book.

The way to *brahman*-realization is re-exposed in the concluding passages of the *Upanishad* with reference to the warranted liberation of one's desires and cutting of "the knots of the heart":

> When are liberated all
> The desires that lodge in one's heart
> Then a mortal becomes immortal
> Therein he reaches *Brahman*
> When are cut all
> The knots of the heart here on earth
> Then a mortal becomes immortal
> –Thus far is the instruction.[31]

For a man who has realized supreme truth (*paramartha-darsi*), explains Sankara,[32] all desires (*kamah*) are broken to pieces, then the unenlightened man, who was mortal, becomes immortal. This is a matter of enlightenment because intellect (*buddhi*) is the seat of desires and resolves, not the self (*atman*). One becomes immortal, by virtue of overcoming death consisting of ignorance, cravings and deeds (*avidya, kamah* and *karma*). Sankara expresses it so beautifully: "death, which causes departure, having been destroyed, there remains no possibility of departure."[33] In other words, ignorance of our kinship with all that is, of the knowledge that the core of our being is indestructible, our inability to restrain desires and reckless doing of deeds in subservience to cravings (*karma* cumulative of demerit), all make death terrible for us. But one who is well rehearsed in keeping these passions at bay, dwells in *brahman* and becomes *brahman*. For such a one there is no death in the sense that death is a superficial affair for one who is not attached to *samsara*.

Sankara interprets "knots of the heart" as concepts arising from ignorance (*avidya*) such as "I am this body," "this wealth in mine," "I am happy or unhappy." When these bondages of *avidya* are destroyed by the knowledge of the identity

---

31 *KU*, VI-14, 15.
32 *SB*, p. 228.
33 *SB*, p. 229.

of *atman* and *brahman*, or of "I am unworldly *brahman*," indeed, then right here (*iha*), in this lifetime, one becomes immortal, explains Sankara.[34] "Thus far this instruction" (*anusasan*) might mean "this is the crux of the teaching of all Vedanta texts" or it may as well be indicative of the conclusion of an original version of the *Katha Upanishad*, to which three more stanzas were added later, as Radhakrishnan informs.[35]

Thus, the *Upanishad* clearly states that when one gives up or restrains voluntarily the incessant demands and cravings of the heart which bind one to a thoughtless worldly existence, then one is ready for the glimpse of and partaking of immortality in this very life. For when these ties with the world are loosened, death ceases to be a radical event or a fearful prospect. Dwelling in the assurance of the indestructibility of one's true self is like dwelling as an immortal.

This is also the moment when one's mind is ready for fundamental knowledge as matters of Being, human existence and meaning of reality assume great importance. It is as if ideas become more real than the things of the visible world. This is also the moment when the philosopher is ready for philosophy.

Kabir on Death and *Bhakti*

The *Katha Upanishad* as a seminal text of the Vedic thanatology influenced generations of Indian philosophers. Some thinkers, from Sankara, Ramanuja and Madhava all the way to modern scholars have been impressed with thoughtful and creative readings of the text and have written philosophical commentaries on it. Others are indirectly influenced by it through the importance they assign to death-contemplation in their work and in their respective creative enrichments of the Vedic tradition. The *bhakti* poet and Hindu saint Kabir (1440–1518), who purposely avoided the path of scholarship and chose the way of *bhakti* (devotion) belongs to this second category.

Kabir's work, handed down to us in the form of songs, *salokas* and *dohas* (quadrates and couplets), offers numerous references to death, the desirable awareness of death and the desirability of practicing a living of death. In other words, Kabir offers us some lucid insights on the subject of death-contemplation and its connection with contemplative living. His insights on this important human possibility lie buried in his poems and couplets, free of scholarly jargon and dogmatic overtones.

The fifth *saloka* in the work of Kabir in the *Adi Granth* seems to sum up the ancient insight of the *Katha Upanishad*:

> Kabir, a rare one is he who dies while living
> Fearless he dwells in the glory of *brahman*
> And *brahman* he encounters whichever way he glances.[36]

---

34 *SB*, p. 230.
35 *RK*, p. 647.
36 *Salok Kabir Je Ke* [The Couplets of Kabir] from *The Adi Granth*, translation mine, *Saloka* 5.

That is, some rare thoughtful individuals willingly practised the death of what people call " the good life" and this practice brings them to a realization that *brahman* is the soul of everything one encounters in the physical world.

Similarly, he says in *Saloka* 22:

Kabir, death that the world is afraid of, brings me joy
Supreme bliss one attains only upon dying.[37]

It is dying of a sort, the same dying that Socrates prescribed as the mark of a true philosopher and the *Katha Upanishad* describes as practiced by Naciketas, which brings us closer to our higher contemplative possibilities. The knowledge of *brahman*, the supreme joy (*ananda*) may be ours in such dying intermingled with contemplation.

In *Saloka* 29 of the *Adi Granth*, Kabir says:

O Kabir, the world is dying, but does not know how to die
So we must die that no more dying there be.[38]

Each time *maya* is chosen over *brahman*, contemplative possibilities are wasted. In the world, dying again and again is happening in this sense as well, there are numerous actual deaths. But the art of dying authentically is seldom embraced. If one dies the voluntary death of *maya*, there will be no more death to strike us. We will be fearless against death and deaths of reincarnations will cease as well. The thoughtful consideration of death has to do with a thoughtful stock-taking of one's endless cravings and ceaseless aspirations to possess this or that in the world of *maya*. Kabir sends the message of the desirability for contemplative living which is but a practice of dying to what is usually termed "the good life" by the *maya*-ridden individuals. It is a cultivation of moderation not a suppression of genuine needs of the body. Nor is it an embracing of actual death by suicide.

An Eastern Classic on Death

The connection between death and the contemplative life is remarkably lucid in the *Katha Upanishad*, which also provides us with a basic outline of the philosophy of the Vedas, with an introduction to the fundamental concepts of the tradition. The legend of Naciketas makes a symbolic statement on the issue of death and philosophy. Naciketas is the genuine philosopher who seeks the meaning of reality *vis-à-vis* death. He is the death-contemplator who knocks at the door of death to seek resolutions of his philosophical problems. Death is shown as the granter of boons to philosophers. The evocation of death is a prerequisite to arrive at that wider canvas on which philosophical problems stand out in relief. Death is the muse of philosophy, as

37 Ibid., *Saloka* 22.
38 Ibid., *Saloka* 29.

Schopenhauer says. It was indeed the starting point of Naciketas' inquiry. The *Katha Upanishad* has seldom been interpreted on the issue of death and philosophy per se or in comparison with Plato's *Phaedo*. Not just the literal rendering of philosophical arguments contained within these texts but reading between the lines, we must dwell on the character sketches of the protagonists and symbolic and dramatic messages of these classics.

In the Vedic world-view, the ideal death indeed is the death of *moha* (attachment) with *maya* (illusory worldliness). It is the same death of "matters bodily" that Socrates prescribed for the philosopher. Since death-contemplation inspires contemplation as such and creates suitable conditions for philosophy to emerge, it should not be taken as leading to a standard outlook on reality. Socrates, Schopenhauer, Heidegger, the ancient author of the *Katha Upanishad* and Kabir all realize the merit of death-contemplation and practice it to compose their respective philosophical systems. But that does not make their systems fully comparable in their contents. Though Socrates and the *Katha Upanishad* are both pioneers in exposing the role of death-contemplation and do so in a remarkably similar way, Platonism and Vedanta remain distinct systems.

Just as Socrates upholds a constant effort on the part of the philosopher to free his or her thought and live "as far as possible" from "matters bodily," similarly Yama's instruction to Naciketas exposes the rewards of a renunciation of *maya* and *moha*. A picture is painted in both the *Phaedo* and the *Katha Upanishad* of the contemplative life and its merits fully exposed. The existential and ontological gains of the practitioner of death are outlined in both these texts. Both expose the meaning of the kind of dying that the contemplative person constantly undergoes. It is not an embracing of actual death (that is, suicide), but a realization of the other life in this very life. Socrates describes it as "soul's dwelling in its own place alone, as in another life, so also in this."[39] The *Katha Upanishad* calls it a passing-on (*samparaye*) not apparent to the childish who are driven by the assumption "this is the only world there is no other,"[40] that is, those absorbed in the world of *maya*. Both Socrates and the *Katha Upanishad* declare this matter hard to understand, contemplation of death is easily misunderstood as an obsession with and seeking of actual death. Socrates in response to Cebes remarks that "people have not [really] found out either in what sense the true philosopher is moribund and deserves death, or what manner of death he deserves."[41] The *Katha Upanishad* calls it the "boon that has entered into the hidden" that has to do with passing-on (*samparaye*) from *avidya* to *vidya*.[42] Furthermore, both the *Phaedo* and the *Katha Upanishad* not only describe the character and the quests of a genuine philosopher, but paint the living portraits of the heroic death-contemplators Socrates and Naciketas.

---

39 Plato, *Phaedo*,. Benjamin Jowett (trans.), in *The Dialogues of Plato* (Chicago, IL: Encyclopaedia Britannica, 1950), 67c, (subsequently, *Phaedo*).

40 *KU*, II-6.

41 *Phaedo,* 64b.

42 *KU*, 1-29.

Since genuine philosophizing must be done in a state of leisure, bodily and mental distractions, worldly anxieties, timely considerations, as well as fragmentary conceptual entrappings must be kept at bay. A philosopher needs relentless practice in living and in thought to seek the fundamentals of reality and to generalize about the nature of things. The death that the philosopher practices is the death of the current and prevalent "answers" that constitute the horizon of accepted worldly meanings, since these answers fall short of being philosophical explanations. Death-contemplation enables one to transcend ever-enticing worldliness, familiar patterns and accepted metaphysical casts of thinking. It creates proper conditions for a fundamental, freer and purer thinking. It enables one to contemplate the "wholes" of life and fundamentals of reality unperturbed by *maya* and matters bodily. The classics of the leading philosophical traditions of the world contain within their expositions of an ideal philosophical and contemplative life unmistakable references to the bond between philosophy and death. A thoughtful acknowledgement of death must evoke a voluntary dying of another kind, that is, living a life of denial and renunciation of excessive worldliness. It is a life best suited to an authentic philosopher, nay, it is even a prerequisite for genuine philosophizing. *Phaedo* and the *Katha Upanishad* say this with one voice. Schopenhauer heeds this call from his western as well as eastern forefathers and incorporates this into his own calling as a philosopher.

Chapter 3

Schopenhauer: Book IV of *The World as Will and Representation*

The connection between death, philosophy and the contemplative life is not only emphasized but thoroughly embedded in Schopenhauer's system. He elucidates this connection in simple but powerful assertions which provide us with gems of insights on the issue of death, contemplation and philosophy. "Indeed without death men will scarcely philosophize" (*The World as Will and Representation*[1], Vol. II, 463; subsequently, *WWR* or *W*) is said with a conviction that penetrates Schopenhauer's own philosophical project. "Death is the real inspiring genius or the muse of philosophy" is a statement that leaps out of his philosophical as well as popular works. "All religions and philosophical systems are … primarily the antidote to the certainty of death" certainly applies this thinker's own system.

Thus, Schopenhauer heeds the call of Socrates in many ways and interprets the bond between death-contemplation, genuine philosophizing and philosophical living with his original terminology as part of his basic quest to elucidate the role of will *vis-à-vis* representation in the human being's world. By embracing the Socratean view of philosophy as a contemplation that characterizes a critical distance and a moral freedom from the excesses of worldly existence, Schopenhauer explains anew why and in which manner the awareness of death is central to the activity of philosophizing as well as to a life led in the shade of philosophical truths at which one has arrived. In this chapter, our task is twofold: (i) we will examine Schopenhauer's *WWR* to outline the role of death-contemplation in it, and (ii) we will expose Schopenhauer's explicit and implicit response to the questions concerning the connection between death, philosophy and contemplative life. Some of these questions can be spelled out as follows: what has death to do with philosophy? Why is death called the muse of philosophy? What sort of contemplative life is outlined and upheld in Schopenhauer's works? Why is suicide dismissed as inconsistent with death-contemplation?

The current expositions of Schopenhauer's thought concerning death for the most part do not focus on the above-mentioned issues. Instead, Schopenhauer's standpoint on the possibility of human immortality or the imperishability of human being's inner nature (will-to-live) have received more attention in many of the available commentaries than the issue of why and how this thinker treats the connection between death, philosophy and an ideal philosophical life. Several

---

1 Quotations from E.F.J. Payne, trans. *The World as Will and Representation* (Dover, 1969) are reprinted with kind permission of the publisher.

studies on the topic of Schopenhauer and death rely either exclusively or too much on a single supplementary essay from Volume II of the *WWR*, namely, "On Death and its Relation to the Indestructibility of Our Inner Nature." Thus the role and the status of death-contemplation in Schopenhauer's entire corpus of philosophical writings have seldom been traced. Due to such sketchy and partial readings of Schopenhauer's work, the aim of his own contemplation on death is heretofore only partially and inadequately exposed as several of his oft-repeated claims are woefully misunderstood. No claim is more misunderstood than Schopenhauer's assertion that "at bottom, we are something that ought not to be; therefore we cease to be ... Death is the great reprimand that the will-to-live ... and egoism ... receive; and it can be conceived as a punishment for our existence" (*W*, II, 507). Due to a misunderstanding of Schopenhauer's unique but radical standpoint as well as due to a misunderstanding of his sympathies with eastern thought, such statements have often been dismissed as indications of his deep-rooted pessimism or as inconsistencies within his fundamental standpoints. For Schopenhauer's treatment, in his works, of his conviction that "at bottom we are something that ought not to be" should not be exposed in a cavalier manner. The ontological as well as ethical implications of this pre-supposition penetrates the entire system of Schopenhauer. The denial of the will-to-live is not merely his recommendation for a contemplative life but also something he himself strove to live by. Whether he did so authentically or inauthentically is a matter that has suffered from the sweeping judgments of his biographers.

We will begin our account of Schopenhauer's thought on the issues of death, contemplation and contemplative life with an exposition of what this thinker maintains concerning these in his relevant and major philosophical works. Our account will also attempt to show how his view of philosophy and his system on the whole embrace death as the most philosophical of all thought-provoking issues. We will also briefly comment on Schopenhauer's own attempts to live a contemplative life with their tragi-comic outcomes.

Perhaps the most obvious and the most important indication of the role of death in Schopenhauer's system is the way he spells out his central concept, namely, the will-to-live. It is the recognition of this will and its blind, incessant urge to live and live it up at all costs, which, according to Schopenhauer, necessitates philosophy. This inner essence can possibly be identified and questioned in case of human beings whereas in animals as well as inanimate entities it remains a blind tendency. The awareness of death, that "terrifying certainty ... that necessarily appears along with the faculty of reason" (*W*, II, 463), must clash with the will-to-live, obliging reason to deal with this certainty, one way or the other. One may either deceive oneself in evading or dismissing this knowledge and remain in unquestioned subservience to the will or alternatively, begin to contemplate the nature of existence and choose a contemplative life that denies the excessive demands of the will-to-live. Thus the exposition of the assertion and denial of the will-to-live form the major themes of *WWR* and to these more than half of the text of Volume I, and supplementary essays of Volume II are explicitly devoted. These themes are crucial to the project of the entire book, for the discussions of the primacy of the will appear in all parts of the book. Since these very themes have intimately to do with the reality, awareness and meaning of death, the contemplation of death remains the muse of Schopenhauer's own philosophical system. This is the chief reason that Schopenhauer refers to and traces the implications of death so frequently in his writings.

The Contemplative Life or the Denial of the Will

In the fourth and final book of Volume I of *WWR*, Schopenhauer discusses what seems to be his outline of a desired contemplative life for one who is determined to overcome the illusory, common and thoughtless existence at the beck and call of the will-to-live. This contemplative life is characterized by an heroic denial of the will-to-live, such denial being an essential component of wisdom. Schopenhauer warns at the outset of this section that although it is convenient to designate these final considerations as "practical philosophy" and the content of the previous three books as "theoretical philosophy," he does not intend this discussion of the possibilities of the denial of the will-to-live to be a prescriptive philosophy or a mere guide to an ideal conduct. It is not an attempt to teach virtue for "virtue is as little taught as is genius," nor is it an effort to outline an "unconditioned ought" in the Kantian fashion. For

> ... all philosophy is always theoretical, since it is essential to it always to maintain a purely contemplative attitude, whatever be the immediate object of investigation; to inquire, not to prescribe ... [Furthermore] it is indeed a palpable contradiction to call the will free and yet to prescribe for it laws by which it is to will ... The will is not only free but even almighty; from it comes not only its action but also its world; and as the will is, so does its action appear, so does its world appear; both are its self-knowledge and nothing more. [*W*, I, 271, 272]

Thus philosophy can only interpret and explain human action and seek to bring the innermost nature of the phenomena of the world to a distinct and abstract knowledge. Schopenhauer is determined to disregard the philosophical "cloud-cuckoo-land" of the "absolute," the "infinite," the "supersensuous," and so on, as well as the (Hegelian) ambition that the nature of the world can be "historically" comprehended: "This actual world of what is knowable, in which we are and which is in us, remains both the material and the limit of our consideration" (*W*, I, 273).

To begin this final consideration of common and mundane human conduct against the possibility of salvation in the sense of liberation from the thoughtless and excessive affirmation of the will-to-live, Schopenhauer makes some preliminary remarks, in sections 54 and 55, about the nature of the will-to-live and death, which are later fully developed in the supplementary essay "On Death and its Relation to the Indestructibility of Our Inner Nature" in Volume II of *WWR*. Although, in order to determine the fuller significance of Schopenhauer's thanatology, we must primarily focus on his outline of the lessons and existential implications of death rather than the nature and/or the aftermath of death, including his convictions concerning the immortality of our essential nature. Some acquaintance with his exposition of the connection between the will-to-live and death is of vital importance. The essential nature of the will and its connection with "life" is explained as follows:

> The will considered purely in itself, is devoid of knowledge and is only a blind, irresistible urge ... Through the addition of the world as representation, developed for its service, the will obtains knowledge of its own willing and what it wills, namely that this is nothing but this world, life, precisely as it exists. We have therefore called the phenomenal world, the mirror, the objectivity, of the will; and as what will wills is always life, just because this is nothing but the presentation of that willing for representation, it is immaterial and a mere pleonasm if, instead of simply saying "the will" we say "the will-to-live" ...
> If will exists, then life, the world will exist. Therefore life is certain to the will-to-live .... [*W*, I, 275]

According to Schopenhauer, the will-to-live is obviously unaffected by the birth and death of individuals as well as arising and perishing of the manifold entities of the world. The observation of the way nature operates leads Schopenhauer to conclude that nature is primarily concerned with the preservation of the species "since she provides for this so lavishly through the immense surplus of the seed and the great strength of the fructifying impulse" (*W*, I, 276). However, nature does not seem to value the individual "who is not only exposed to destruction in a thousand ways from the most insignificant accidents but is even destined for this and led toward it by nature herself"(*W*, I, 276). Even nature seems to convey that only the Ideas (species), not individuals are real and constitute the objectivity of the will.

Thus, the will-to-live being the inner core of man and man being the highest grade of the self-consciousness of this will, the immortality of the will must mean indestructibility of man's inner nature. In other words, man must partake in the deathlessness of the will-to-live. This permanence of man's inner core does not mean that our individuality is carried over beyond death as some naïve accounts of immortality may seem to assert. Schopenhauer explains not only the kind of immortality that human beings can assure themselves of, but also traces the meaning and implications of death for human existence both in Book IV of *WWR* as well as in various supplementary essays pertaining to this book in Volume II.

The imperishableness of the species and transitoriness of the individuals indicate that nourishment and renewal among individuals is comparable to generation and death to excretion. To embalm corpses is tantamount to a careful preservation of excreta (*W*, I, 277). As part of nature's aim to preserve the species, death of the body and the cessation of the individuality is as natural and normal as going to the toilet. Death is also comparable to deep sleep, for "death is a sleep in which individuality is forgotten, everything else awakens again or rather has remained awake" (*W*, I. 278). The truth that there is death awakens in us the realization that the thing-in-itself that constitutes us also objectifies itself in everything that there is. Death is a warning against egoism, as Schopenhauer explains in his supplementary essay:

Egoism really consists in man's restricting all reality to his own person, in that he imagines he lives in this alone, and not in others. Death teaches him something better, since it abolishes this person, so that man's true nature, that is his will, will henceforth live only in other individuals ... for the difference between external and internal ceases. [*W*, II, 507]

It is an amazing thing that whereas all human beings are aware that they are destined to die, they live and go about their daily tasks as if they were not so aware. How can we so easily dismiss and sideline the fact of our own death? Schopenhauer's metaphysics of the will explains this mystery:

In man as in animal that does not think, there prevails as a lasting state of mind the certainty springing from innermost consciousness that he is nature, the world itself. By virtue of this no one is noticeably disturbed by the thought of certain and never distant death, but everyone lives on as though he is bound to live forever. Indeed this is true to the extent that it might be said that no one has a really lively conviction of the certainty of his death, as otherwise there could not be a very great difference between his frame of mind and that of the condemned criminal. Everyone recognizes that certainty in the abstract and theoretically, but lays it on one side like other theoretical truths that are not applicable in practice, without taking it into his vivid consciousness ... [For] this peculiarity of the human way of thinking methods of explaining it from habit and acquiescence in the inevitable are by no means sufficient ... the reason for it is deeper. The same thing can also explain why at all times and among all peoples dogmas of some kind, dealing with the individual's continued existence after death, exist and are highly esteemed. [*W*, I, 282]

Schopenhauer attributes human self-assurance in the face of death to a deeper instinctual conviction in our Being or a gut feeling that something in us is imperishable and always endowed with a "present". This vital force in us, which Schopenhauer calls the will to live, and not any reasoning is responsible for the calmness with which we face the issue of personal death. The truth of death is for the most part laid aside as a theoretical truth "not applicable in practice." Tolstoy, in his celebrated short story "Death of Ivan Ilyich," graphically illustrates the initial non-acceptance of his impending death by the hero of this narrative, as he clearly recognizes the truth of the syllogism "all men are mortal, Socrates is a man, therefore, Socrates is mortal," but cannot accept that he himself, the little Vanya as he was called in his childhood, is mortal and due and expected to die soon enough. To explain this calmness toward death in terms of habit and acquiescence in the inevitable is unacceptable in Schopenhauer's view. Heidegger seems to attribute this evasion of death to an inauthentic habituation to be surmounted by an authentic contemplation (anticipation) of death. According to Schopenhauer, such tranquility against death is part and parcel of man being an animal, and the inner conviction of the will concerning its own immortality.

This gut feeling concerning the permanence of will does not prevent the fear of death which may grip someone in the face of a mortal threat or an imagined and depressive brooding over death. Schopenhauer clarifies that pain and death are two different evils. We do not fear pain involved in death. What one fears in death is the ending of one's individuality; that is, the ending of a particular objectification of the will-to-live, death being the threat to will-to-live if a particular entity is resisted by the full force of the individual. However, the faculty of reasoning can enable us to consider the whole instead of the particular.

In Book IV of the *WWR*, Schopenhauer explains both the ongoing and often uncontemplated affirmation as well as the possibility of the denial of the will-to-live: "To exhibit both and to bring them to the distinct knowledge of the faculty of reason can be my only aim, and not to prescribe or recommend the one or the other, which would be as foolish as it would be pointless" (*W*, I, 285).

This is consistent with Schopenhauer's view that will is free, how to wish cannot be learnt and virtue cannot be learnt and cannot be taught. He is never tired of quoting from classical sources to this effect. However, more light needs to be shed on the freedom and necessity pertaining to the will-to-live and his adoration of those who lead the holy life of the denial of the will. Schopenhauer does seem to recommend a dose of such denial to all contemplative individuals. Schopenhauer's own life shows various and repeated attempts to deny what is known as a customary and middle-class life of civic virtue. The affirmation and denial of the will-to-live are defined as follows in Section 54:

> The will affirms itself; this means that while in its objectivity, that is to say, in the world and in life, its own inner nature is completely and distinctly given to it as representation, this knowledge does not in any way impede its willing. It means that just this life thus known is now willed as such by the will with knowledge, consciously and deliberately, just as hitherto the will willed it without knowledge and as a blind impulse.

> The opposite of this, "the denial of the will to live," shows itself when willing ends with that knowledge, since the particular phenomena known then no longer act as "motives" of willing, but the whole knowledge of the inner nature of the world that mirrors the will, knowledge that has grown up through apprehension of the Ideas, because the "quieter" of the will, and thus the will freely abolishes itself. [*W*, I, 285]

Schopenhauer explicates the unique human possibility of the denial of the will with elucidations of freedom and necessity the three levels of human character, namely the intelligible, empirical and acquired, as well as motivations and decisions of the will in Section 55. This possibility, as well as the phenomena of asceticism and holiness, are further traced in the examples of some Christian mystics as well as Hindu, Buddhist and Sufi saints and mystics. The lives of these wise men demonstrate the practice of the denial of the will-to-live, their different religious persuasions notwithstanding.

One of the implications of the fact that the will is free is that through its most complete phenomenon endowed with knowledge, that is, man, it is even able to deny itself. That the will as such is free is a logical outcome of Schopenhauer's view that it is the thing-in-itself, for it is the ultimate ground of all phenomena and itself having no further ground. The phenomena, as the objectification of the will, are subject to the principle of sufficient reason; the will itself is not. However, the freedom of the will is fully actualized only in man, an entity "illuminated by so high a degree of knowledge that even a perfectly adequate repetition of the inner nature of the world under the form of the representation becomes possible in it ... [that is,] the apprehension of the ideas, the pure mirror of the world" (*W*, I, 288). Thus, it is possible for the will to acquire through man full self-consciousness, distinct and fundamental knowledge of its inner nature as evidenced in the whole world: "Through the same knowledge an elimination and self-denial of the will in its most perfect phenomenon is possible" (*W*, I, 288). Thus, due primarily to this possibility not just the will but man too may be called free, and distinguished thereby from all other entities. Schopenhauer says, however, that man being free in this sense does not mean that particular human actions are not subject to any necessity, or that the motives and character have no bearing on them.

Schopenhauer also explains that his concept of the will is not the same as the will which was taken as an act of thought and identified with judgment in modern philosophy especially by Descartes and Spinoza. The modern concept is a by-product of the Greek doctrine that finds man's inner nature in the *soul*, which was understood as being originally a "knowing" as well as a "thinking" entity, and only as a result of this, a willing entity. Schopenhauer presents his own radically untraditional insight as follows:

> According to the whole of my fundamental view, all this is a reversal of the true relation. The will is first and original; knowledge is merely added to if as an instrument belonging to the phenomenon of the will ... With those other thinkers [man] wills what he knows; with me, he knows what he wills. [*W*, I, 293]

Schopenhauer obviously takes pride in his departure from the traditional and strictly rational view of the essence of a human being. He fully acknowledges the paramount status of will as the Being of the human entity, something that humans share with all entities, and at the same time acknowledges the role of the "instinct" as well as that of the "body" *vis-à-vis* the soul. The role of "knowledge" is also recognized. Although for the most part it is consumed by the service of the will, it also contains the possibility of a denial of the will-to-live, as cited above, it is "the whole knowledge of the inner nature of the world that mirrors the will ... becomes the quieter of the will and thus the will freely abolishes itself" (*W*, I, 285).

With respect to the will's aim and object, Schopenhauer identifies striving as its basic nature, for "striving is its sole nature to which no attained goal can put an end. Such striving is therefore incapable of satisfaction" (*W*, I, 308). All hindrance to the will's striving, or obstacles placed between the will and its temporary goal, is called "suffering" by Schopenhauer: "Thus that there is no ultimate aim of striving means that there is no measure or end of suffering" (*W*, I, 309).

At the higher grades of the objectifications of the will, it "appears as a living body with the iron command to nourish it. What gives force to this command is just that this body is nothing but the objectified will-to-live itself. Man, as the most complete objectification of this will, is accordingly the most necessitous of all beings" (*W*, I, 312). Schopenhauer is never tired of reminding us that as soon as man receives a bit of a respite from want and suffering, boredom strikes him. Almost all men who become secure from want and cares become "a burden to themselves, after having finally cast off all other burdens" (*W*, I, 313). A temporary releasement from the strivings of the will come to those who are capable of purely intellectual pleasures:

> What might otherwise be called the finest part of life, its purest joy, just because it lifts us out of real existence and transforms us into disinterested spectators of it, is pure knowledge which remains foreign to all willing, pleasure in the beautiful, genuine delight in art. But because this requires rare talents, it is granted only to extremely few, and even to those as a fleeting dream. [*W*, I, 314]

This account of human suffering given in Sections 56–9 is elaborated upon so frequently in Schopenhauer's later philosophical as well as popular works that it has earned him the title of "the pessimistic philosopher." This categorization of his philosophical outlook often casts a cloud over a genuine appreciation of his original philosophical insights.

The reason that Schopenhauer takes suffering to be a positive phenomenon and what is commonly called "happiness" essentially negative only is exposed as follows by him:

> Frequently we shut our eyes to the truth, comparable to a bitter medicine that suffering is essential to life and therefore does not flow in upon us from outside, but that everyone carries around within himself its perennial source. On the contrary, we are constantly looking for a particular external cause, as it were a pretext for the pain that never leaves us, just as the free man makes for himself an idol, in order to have a master. [*W*, I, 318]

After having explained the freedom of the will as well as the necessity of its phenomenon, Schopenhauer outlines the affirmation and the denial of the will more specifically:

> The affirmation of the will is the persistent willing itself. Undisturbed by any knowledge, as it fills the life of man in general. For the body of man is already the objectivity of the will, as it appears at this grade and in this individual; and thus, his willing that develops in time is, so to speak, the paraphrase of the body, the elucidation of the meaning of the whole and of its parts. It is another way of exhibiting the same thing-in-itself of which the body is already the phenomenon. Therefore, instead of affirmation of the will we can also say affirmation of the body. The fundamental theme of all the many different acts of will is the satisfaction of the needs inseparable from the body's existence in health, they have their expression in it, and can be reduced to the maintenance of the individual and the propagation of the race. [*W*, I, 327]

The affirmation of the will is the persistent willing unhindered by the commands of pure knowledge. This incessant willing is in a way a paraphrase of the body, for the body is an objectification of the will, albeit a particular manifestation of it. Thus, the affirmation of the will can be called the affirmation of the body. Schopenhauer seems to endorse the Socratean attitude toward the body, that is, body as a symbol of the excessive and thoughtless worldliness, willing, he describes as the "paraphrase of the body." The common and basic theme of the different acts of will is the satisfaction of the needs of the body, the maintenance of the individual and the propagation of the race. The above passage of Schopenhauer's seems to be reiteration of what Socrates is reported to have said in the *Phaedo*:

> For the body is a source of endless trouble to us by reason of the mere requirement of food; and is liable also to diseases which overtake and impede us in the search after true Being: it fills us full of loves and lusts and fears and fancies of all kinds and endless foolery, and in fact, as men say, takes away from us the power of thinking at all. Whence come wars, and fightings, and factions? Whence but from the body and lusts of the body? Wars are occasioned by the love of money, and money has to be acquired for the sake and in the service of the body; and by reason of all these impediments we have no time to give to philosophy.[2]

The service of the body or what Schopenhauer calls "the affirmation of the will" comes as a matter of course to the human being and knowledge remains subordinated to willing unless a knowledge of another kind appears which recognizes the lusts and motives of all willing. This is the philosophical knowledge that denies common willing and thoughtless subservience to the body. For the most part, however, human beings fail to recognize the subordination of their knowledge to their ceaseless willing:

> From the first appearance of his consciousness, man finds himself to be a willing being, and his knowledge, as a rule remains in constant relation to his will. He tries to become thoroughly acquainted only with the objects of his willing, and then with the means to attain these. Now he knows what he has to do, and does not as a rule aim at other knowledge. [*W*, I, 327]

Being preoccupied in the pursuit of the objects of their willing, human beings seldom have time for "the other knowledge":

> It is always an exception when such a life suffers an interruption through the fact that either the aesthetic demand for contemplation or the ethical demand for renunciation proceeds from a knowledge independent of the service of the will, and directed to the inner nature of the world in general. (*W*, I, 328).

This contemplative renunciation or death-contemplation, which is certainly a human possibility, happens but scarcely. For the most part the mind is entrapped in the permutations and combinations of the agenda of the will to live: "This is the life of almost all men; they will, they know what they will, and they strive after this with enough success to protect them from despair, and enough failure to preserve them from boredom and its consequences" (*W*, I, 327).

According to Schopenhauer, the intensity of the will manifests itself in the sexual impulse. This impulse represents the "most decided affirmation of the will to live." It is by this act that "every species of living thing is bound to a whole and perpetuated as

---

2   Plato, *Phaedo*, 66, b.

such" (*W*, I, 328). The satisfaction of the sexual impulse is not merely the affirmation of one's own existence. "It affirms life for an indefinite time beyond the death of the individual" (*W*, I, 328).

The sexual impulse which has been called "the most decided affirmation of the will-to-live" by Schopenhauer represents, according to him, the focal point, the visible expression and vehement manifestation of the will. As explained at length in his supplementary essay "The Metaphysics of Sexual Love" (*W*, II, 531), the sexual impulse is not merely an individual's own urge, but something part and parcel of a grand purpose of the will to propagate the species to which the individual belongs. Unbeknownst to the lovers, their romantic love is a fulfillment of the will's purpose, and romantic love is, at bottom, a sexual attraction, according to Schopenhauer:

> Nature too, the inner being of which is will-to-live itself with all her force impels both man and animal to propagate. After this she has attained her end with the individual, and is quite indifferent to its destruction, for as the will-to-live she is concerned only with the preservation of the species; the individual is nothing to her. [*W*, I, 330]

This is why the denial of the will-to-live requires first and foremost, a closer study, control, regulation and even suppression of one's sexual impulse. Schopenhauer treats such a suppression of sexuality as part and parcel of saying no to the will-to-live and seems to admire the sexual restraint of those who chose an ascetical and saintly way of life. As we shall see, this account of sexuality and of asceticism may be a glaring oversimplification. Whereas a close connection between the sexual impulse and the human being's thoughtless worldliness cannot be denied, Schopenhauer certainly turns a blind eye to the middle course of moderation that is celebrated in ancient philosophical systems and religions alike. Schopenhauer traces a connection between "genitals" and "generation" to reaffirm his view of sexuality:

> Far more than any other external member of the body the genitals are subject merely to the will and not at all to knowledge. Here, in fact, the will shows itself independent of knowledge as it does in those parts which, on the occasion of mere stimuli, serve vegetative life, reproduction, and in which the will operates blindly as it does in nature without knowledge. [*W*, I, 330]

The psychological aspects of human sexuality, and its deeper connection with love are not analyzed and the issue whether sexuality is more than a mere physical manifestation of the will's purposes is left unexamined in Schopenhauer's account. The body itself is an objectification of willing and genitals more than any other parts represent this objectification. Thus, the relation between willing, worldliness and sexuality is insightfully traced by Schopenhauer. The importance of the unconscious and the omnipresence of sexuality in the psychical and the practical life of the human entity was recognized by Schopenhauer in no uncertain terms. These insights influenced several later thinkers and psychologists in the European tradition including Nietzsche, Freud, Thomas Mann and others. In a discussion of Schopenhauer's possible influence on Freud, Bryan Magee writes:

In his analysis of the importance of sex in human life Schopenhauer was an intrepid pioneer who held ideas far ahead of his time. Jung was directly influenced by him, and two outstanding authorities on sex – Ellis and Bloch – admired him greatly and cited him frequently ... Freud was familiar with these ideas and considered them of great value ... Freud ... never, in his maturity equivocated over the fact that Schopenhauer had preceded him with his most fundamental ideas, but only over the directness or indirectness of his debt.[3]

It is quite clear in Schopenhauer's analysis that any denial of thoughtless and matter-of-course worldliness requires a denial or rejection or overcoming of the sexual drive which is but will's most remarkable manifestation. If sexuality has intimately to do with denial, then it also has a deep-rooted connection with death and death-contemplation. An elucidation of the connection between sexuality and death is one of the most remarkable insights of Schopenhauer's thought, even though the possibility of moderation and the middle path is woefully missing in this account.

Egoism and Eternal Justice

In Book IV of the *WWR*, Schopenhauer reinterprets several fundamental and classical ethical concepts *vis-à-vis* his central notion of the will-to-live. The notions of freedom, suffering, good and bad, right and wrong, intelligible, character (intelligible, empirical and acquired), egoism, temporal and eternal justice, sympathy and several other ethical concepts are all analyzed in terms of the pivotal reality of the will-to-live. All these considerations lead up to the all-important exposition of the denial of the will-to-live. Instead of trying to explicate each and every ethical concept dealt with in Book IV, we shall focus on those conceptual analyses that are relevant to death, contemplation and contemplative life, a life which in Schopenhauerian terms must be seen as the one characterized by the denial of the will-to-live.

The exposition of "egoism" is quite interesting and relevant to the issue of death and contemplation. According to Schopenhauer, egoism reflects itself in the constant struggle and conflict that exists among the individuals within every species, within every grade of the objectification of the will. Human existence which is the highest grade of will's objectification is no exception and shows this conflict among its individuals more distinctly and surely albeit in a more sophisticated and subtle form. Schopenhauer regards egoism as the starting point of all conflict. Time and space, being the essential forms of knowledge that originates from the will, are called *principium individuationis* through which the will manifests itself in the plurality of individuals. Since will is present within each individual,

> everyone wants everything for himself, wants to possess, or at least control everything, and would like to destroy whatever opposes him. In addition, there is in the case of knowing beings the fact that the individual is the bearer of the knowing subject, and this

3   Bryan Magee, *The Philosophy of Schopenhauer* (New York: Oxford University Press, 1997), p. 309.

knowing subject is the bearer of the world ... Every knowing individual is therefore in truth, and finds himself as, the whole will-to-live, or as the in-itself of the world itself, and also as the complementary condition of the world as representation, consequently as a microcosm to be valued equally with the macrocosm. [*W*, I, 332]

This is the reason, says Schopenhauer, that every individual regards himself the center of the world. This knowledge in its simplicity and immediate certainty exists in every individual and exists independently of and prior to all reflection:

But it is precisely through [this] egoism that will's inner conflict with itself attains to such fearful revelation ... At one time we see it from its dreadful side in the lives of great tyrants and evildoers, and in world-devastating wars. On another occasion we see its ludicrous side where it is the theme of comedy, and shows itself particularly in self-conceit and vanity. [*W*, I, 333]

The omnipresence of "egoism" is graphically exposed by Schopenhauer, this being the source and manifestation of suffering that he regards as essential to life. Egoism prompts certain individuals to "destroy another's happiness or life in order to increase by an insignificant amount his own well-being." Then there are also instances of real wickedness "that seeks, quite disinterestedly, the pain and injury of others without any advantage to itself." Schopenhauer calls this strife of all individuals, or the inner contradiction of the will with itself, the fundamental source of suffering, essential and inevitable to all life, "in spite of the precautions that have been taken against it." The existence of ethical values as well as of the state and its system of temporal justice and punishment are such precautions that the society takes against the spillover of egoism resulting from the actions of certain egotistical individuals.

The problem of the omnipresence of suffering, especially the suffering caused by reckless egoism is one of the most challenging issues for Schopenhauer. All this suffering, strife and consequences of unbridled egoism may be characterized as the inner conflict of the will. However, fundamental causes of suffering cannot be narrowed down to egoism alone. For a reference to egoism does not fully explain why bad things may happen to good people, why suffering seems to be the rule and happiness an elusive interlude, and a thoughtless subservience to will is to be doomed to be a lower life. A fuller account of suffering must include an exposition of "eternal justice," an interesting but controversial concept in Schopenhauer's thought. This doctrine, which Schopenhauer posits as all important, is either dismissed with the wave of a hand, or called "absurd" and "perverse" by many Schopenhauer scholars of our day. Others, who do give it some attention, woefully misunderstand it.[4] As we shall see in our comprehensive analysis of Schopenhauer's study of eastern thought

---

4   For example, Michael Fox, "Schopenhauer on Death, Suicide and Self-renunciation," in M. Fox (ed.), *Schopenhauer: His Philosophical Achievement* (Sussex: Harvester Press, 1980); David E. Cartwright, "Schopenhauer on Suffering, Death, Guilt and the Consolations of Metaphysics," in Eric von der Luft (ed.), *Schopenhauer: New Essays* (Lewiston, NY: Edwin Mellen Pess); John E. Atwell, *Schopenhauer: The Human Character* (Philadelphia, PA: Temple University Press, 1990).

in Chapter 5, the concepts of eternal justice as well as original sin in Schopenhauer's thought cannot be adequately understood without an intimate grasp of the eastern world-views of Vedanta and Buddhism, with which Schopenhauer is sympathetically involved. He alludes to several eastern concepts and beliefs, in order to elucidate and find support for his own unique and formidable concepts, of which "eternal justice" is one outstanding example.

Before referring to eternal justice and its implications of the existence of suffering, Schopenhauer explains the raison d'être of the state and its system of temporal justice and punishment as society's ways to keep in check the harmful impacts of blind egoism. Eternal justice of course will be posited in contrast with the temporal justice which is superior to mere revenge. Revenge is a tit for tat for a past deed. However, retaliation is a form of evil, for evil cannot be ethically justified. The motivation for punishment meted out by state to a criminal in fulfillment of law, is to prevent and deter criminal acts in the future. Thus, punishment directed at the future is superior to revenge, which is merely a reaction to the past. The relation between egoism, the existence of which has already been explained in terms of the will-to-live, and the state is exposed in his characteristic simple expressions, by Schopenhauer. The state does very little to egoism in general yet "from egoism it has sprung and it exists merely to serve it." In other words, the state is helpless against "the inner disposition to which alone, morality or immorality belongs," yet it is a safeguard or summation of common egoism of all:

> The state is set up on the correct assumption that pure morality, i.e., right conduct from moral grounds is not to be expected; otherwise it itself would be superfluous. Thus the state aiming at well-being, is by no means directed against egoism, but only against the injurious consequences of egoism arising out of the plurality of egoistic individuals, reciprocally affecting them, and disturbing their well-being. [*W*, I, 345]

The state is never entirely successful in its goal of the removal of evil. Nor can it wipe out the dissension and discord among individuals, for human beings suffer and irritate each other in trifles, petty politics and unnecessary social conflict, once they find themselves free of larger evils. Anytime there is freedom from want, boredom never fails to raise its head. The strife often turns outward in the form of wars among nations, exacting bloody sacrifices from states, which might otherwise be enjoying internal peace. In sum, suffering of human life is not a thing that can be eliminated by any formal or social measures whatsoever.

There is, however, an "eternal justice," which rules not the state but the world. Schopenhauer is fully convinced of the existence of this essential, ever-present, inner justice in the nature of things, for it is fully compatible with the operations of the will-to-live. This eternal justice exists in many ways in contrast to the temporal justice of the state: "This is not dependent on human institutions not subject to chance and deception, not uncertain, wavering and erring but infallible, firm and certain" (*W*, I, 350). It is not a retributive justice, and does not require, and is not based on, time. Here the punishment and the offence fuse into each other and are one and the same thing. Schopenhauer quotes Euripides "the punishment is already here, if only you would see it" (*W*, I, 351).

Eternal justice is a natural outcome of the way the world is. The world in all its plurality is the phenomenon of the "one" will-to-live. The will pervades everything and being free or self-determining operates in a timeless rather than time-bound fashion. Thus, "every being supports existence in general, and the existence of its species, and of its characteristic individuality … and in all that happens or indeed can happen to the individual, justice is always done to it. For the will belongs to it, and as the will is, so is the world" (*W*, I, 352). Although Schopenhauer posits a fundamental Being of all beings and calls it the will, nonetheless he remains non-theistic and this-worldly in his exposition of reality:

> Only this world itself – no other – can bear the responsibility for its existence and its nature; for how could anyone else have assumed this responsibility. If we want to know what human beings, morally considered, are worth as a whole and in general, let us consider their fate as a whole and in general. This fate is want, wretchedness, misery, lamentation, and death. Eternal justice prevails; if they were not as a whole contemptible, their fate as whole would not be melancholy. In this sense we can say that the world itself is the tribunal of the world. If we could lay all the misery of the world in one pan of the scales, and all its guilt in the other, the pointer will certainly show them to be in equilibrium. [*W*, I, 352]

At first sight, these statements appear to be shocking. It is no wonder that several interpreters of Schopenhauer have been appalled by his radical stance. However, a simple comparison of all this with the law of karma, a well-recognized principle within Vedanta and Buddhism will enable us to make sense out of Schopenhauer's theory of eternal justice.

The omnipresence of the will-to-live gives its objectivity that is the world the status of being self-caused: "Only this world itself—no other—can bear the responsibility for its existence and nature." The references to a creator god, a higher world, heaven and hell do not suffice as an explanation of what transpires in this world. The causes of what happens must be traced in this world alone. And if causes and effects of the human condition are both to be located here in the phenomena of the will-to-live, then this will must have its rhyme and reason in itself. It must operate on an internal lawfulness or an eternal justice. All the apparent sufferings, which clearly outweigh the interludes of happiness undergone by human beings in general, must be in a way owed to them. This world must be the tribunal of this world. All theories of humans deserving their fate such as those of original sin, karma and reincarnation begin to make sense when we accept the notion that this world is its own tribunal. The world itself and being born into it, a return to *samsara* cannot be described as a desirable or happy event because this is precisely from which a release is to be sought by all pursuits of salvation. Thus unbridled optimism and glee is nothing but self-deception according to Schopenhauer.

Moreover, the signs of eternal justice are visible in the human condition itself: "Here the punishment must be so linked with offence that the two are one." Although the myths of the Greeks and the Indians speak of a tablet of Jove, and for Yama *dharmaraja* (the Hindu god of death), who is also the registrar of karma, the "sins of men" must be so innumerable to keep track of and to reserve judgment on them for subsequent punishment. Eternal justice must provide for an instant punishment or reward for deeds done. It is due to this hidden justice that anger, hatred and jealousy feed on their own perpetrator. It is the eternal justice that makes the doing of good its own reward and happiness is found often in making others happy. But the common knowledge of the mortals does not witness eternal justice, for this knowledge is covered by the veil of *maya*, and subserves the will itself; the individual perceives everything in terms of the *principium individuationis* and in the forms of the principle of sufficient reason:

> In this form of his limited knowledge he sees not the inner nature of things, which is one, but its phenomena as separated, detached, innumerable, very different and indeed opposed. For pleasure appears to him as one thing and pain quite another; one man tormentor and murdered, another as martyr and victim, wickedness as one thing, evil as another … He himself in the vehement pressure of will, which is his origin and inner nature, grasps the pleasures and enjoyments of life, embraces them firmly, and does not know that, by this very act of his will, he seizes and hugs all the pains and miseries of life, at the sight of which he shudders … The boundless world everywhere full of suffering in the infinite past, in the infinite future, is strange to him, is indeed a fiction. His vanishing person, his extensionless present, his momentary gratification, these alone have reality for him; and he does everything to maintain them, so long as his eyes are not opened by a better knowledge. [*W*, I, 352–3]

This limited knowledge and the "better knowledge" referred to by Schopenhauer are called *maya* and *jnana* respectively by the Vedanta school of Hindu thought. What *jnana* reveals, first and foremost, is the one-ness of everything that exists and transpires. For *brahman* (divine Being) pervades all entities and *maya* prevents this realization. Self-love or attachment to pleasure or *moha* is an important ingredient of *maya*. Schopenhauer does not invoke the concept of *brahman* (Being) explicitly but does find affinity of his own concepts with those of *maya*, *moha* and *jnana*. And when Schopenhauer applauds the poet Calderon for saying that "man's greatest offence is that he has been born" and remarks on it that "how could it fail to be an offence, as death comes after it in accordance with an eternal law" (*W*, I, 355), he is once again in admiration of Vedantic and Buddhist disdain of *samsara*. The ideas that existence and longing to exist is an offence, and death a lawful punishment for it are not the ravings of a rabid pessimist, but the well-considered thought of a thinker steeped in the ancient wisdom of Christian, Hindu and Buddhist world-views.

Schopenhauer appreciates the rationale behind the notion of original sin and at the same time admires the wisdom behind the necessity to overcome *samsara* as taught by Vedanta and Buddhism. For the first phrase of the first noble truth of the Buddha, namely, that "birth is *dukkha* (pain)," is not very different from what Calderon says, namely, that being born is an offense. Both statements can be dismissed outright as reckless pessimism. But that would be an oversimplification. Those can also be understood as profound depictions of reality. Schopenhauer's rejoinder is equally profound when he says that existence is definitely an offense, for "death comes after it in accordance with an eternal law." Death (including knowledge of an immanent end) as punishment for existing indicates that that existence is tainted. It is not an innocent occurrence. Love of existence makes it ever more tainted for it disregards death, an inevitable punishment for clinging to existence. This profound statement of Schopenhauer's also indicates that the "why" of death can never entirely be answered. That this punishment is in store for everyone without exception reveals that existence on the whole and as such cannot be simplistically described as a gala event, as a gift merely to be relished. In a fuller account of life, death as its destiny must be included. Living must include a kind of not-living in awe of the ultimate not-being.

Schopenhauer advocates the wisdom behind the myth of reincarnation or transmigration of souls, a belief held by three-quarters of humanity:

> The myth makes intelligible the ethical significance of conduct through figurative description in the method of knowledge according to the principle of sufficient reason which is eternally foreign to this significance ... This teaches that all sufferings inflicted in life by man on other beings must be expiated in a following life in this world by precisely the same sufferings ... Never has a myth been, and never will one be, more closely associated with a philosophical truth accessible to so few, than this very teaching of the noblest and the oldest of peoples. [*W*, I, 355, 356]

The philosophical truth that goes hand in hand with this myth is the higher truth of the one-ness of all existence, and the ethical significance of giving up *samsara* voluntarily as far as feasible in this life of flesh. The eternal justice prevails as an authentication of that higher truth and keeps everything in balance.

The essential nature of eternal justice and the unity of will within all phenomena are often known, albeit as obscure feelings to all human beings. Schopenhauer points out that some characteristics of human nature that seem to applaud eternal justice and on occasion, offers self-sacrifice on behalf of it (*W*, I, 357–9). There is a feeling of satisfaction that all of us have when a perpetrator of pain on others suffers in exactly the same measure. Even the persons who are not involved directly seem to applaud poetic justice. Furthermore, we are also greatly impressed by someone who avenges a great outrage, which he has experienced or merely witnessed, all by himself at the cost of his life. It is as if he has made himself the arm of eternal justice, whose true inner nature he does not understand because he is carrying out an act of revenge at the level of the *principium individuationis*. For a higher knowledge of the unity of all phenomena forbids retaliation and revenge. Schopenhauer cites a quote from the Bible indicating that Christian ethics having that higher knowledge, declares all revenge as being outside the province of man: "Vengeance is mine: I will repay, saith the Lord" (Romans xii:19).

The Path of Will-lessness

In the last sections (68–71) of Book IV, Schopenhauer gives us a fuller account of what he calls "the denial of the will-to-live." It is a distinct human possibility to be able to shun the ceaseless oppression of the will's commands and to abide in a state where wisdom or will's knowledge of itself and higher life of self-denial combine to produce a "state of voluntary renunciation, resignation, true composure and complete will-lessness" (*W*, I, 379). Schopenhauer sets up a contrast between a thoughtless, matter-of-course subservience to the will, and rare but determined denial of will's commands. He seems to leave no middle ground between the common affirmation of the will and its complete denial. There are at least four major classical sources upon which Schopenhauer's account of will's denial seems to be based. The life of the denial of the will-to-live has much in common with an authentic attitude toward death, contemplation and the philosophical life that Socrates is reported to have exemplified at the dawn of western thought. He also finds an affinity of his concepts with his own version of New Testament Christianity, along with its concepts of original sin, salvation and grace, a Christianity thoroughly comparable with Hinduism and the Indian spirit. Section 70 is devoted entirely to locating the denial of the will within Christian thought. At the same time he authenticates and illustrates the validity of his concepts and assertions with an ongoing comparison with Vedantic and Buddhist texts. Of course, the later editions of *WWR* have more and more references to the eastern sources and he continues to show his deeper interest and enhanced knowledge of Vedanta and Buddhism in his later writings. Another important source is the biographical accounts of some renowned western mystics, along with some general references to eastern *sufis*, *samanas*, *sadhus* and saints. It was Wilhelm Dilthey who recommended and carried out biographical analyses of the lived-world of philosophers as a way of genuine philosophizing. In his own fusion of philosophizing and living, Schopenhauer seems to have given a demonstration of this way of doing philosophy.

Denial of the will-to-live is the epitome of all wisdom and ethical conduct. For the knowledge of the existence of the same will in all entities, its inner contradiction in egoism, eternal justice and that of will's incessant cravings prompts a thoughtful individual to seek a deliverance from it. Thus after an extended analysis of classical ethical concepts in terms of the will and its possible denial, Schopenhauer remarks: "From the same source from which all goodness, affection, virtue, and mobility of character spring, there ultimately arises what I call denial of the will-to-live" (*W*, I, 378).

This denial of the will is prompted by a "seeing through" the *principium individuationis* or by the lifting of "the veil of *maya*." The realization of "the identity of the will in all its phenomena" has a positive impact. One rises above the common egotistical (and absolute) distinction between oneself and the others. One takes a deep interest in the sufferings of others as if these were one's own. Such a one "takes upon himself the pain of the whole world":

Wherever he looks he sees suffering humanity and the suffering animal world, a world
that passes away ... Now how could he, with such knowledge of the world, affirm this
very life through constant acts of will, and precisely in this way bind himself more and
more firmly to it, press himself to it more and more closely ...

That knowledge of the whole, of the inner nature of the thing-in-itself ... becomes
the quieter of all and every willing. The will now turns away from life; it shudders at
the pleasures in which it recognizes the affirmation of life. Man attains to the state of
voluntary renunciation, resignation, true composure and complete will-lessness. [*W*, I,
379]

This denial of the will-to-live seems to be essentially the same as what we have called
"death-contemplation," or the practice of doing without what is commonly called "the
good life." According to Schopenhauer, there are two mutually connected insights
that lead a thoughtful person to choose the path of will-lessness. The knowledge of
boundless suffering of the human and animal world combined with its transitoriness,
that is, a compassionate acknowledgement and a conscious identification with the
sufferings of others could inspire one to renounce the matter-of-course life of the
will. At the same time, the knowledge of "the inner nature of the thing-in-itself,"
or the rare possibility of the otherwise blind will-to-live becoming self-aware, also
drives one toward a voluntary will-lessness. Only in the human entity, the will has
a possibility to take a pause, become aware of its own machinations and to deny
itself. Schopenhauer mentions this a few times. In the midst of self-contemplation
we arrive at a juncture when:

The hard experience of our own sufferings or in the vividly recognized sufferings of
others, knowledge of the vanity and bitterness of life comes close to us who are still
enveloped in the veil of Maya. We would like to deprive desires of their sting, close the
entry to all suffering, purify and sanctify ourselves by complete and final resignation. [*W*,
I, 379]

One's sensitivity toward one's own actual as well as possible suffering, one's
empathy toward others' sufferings and one's realization of the hard facts of existence
make one question the thoughtless and endless business of chasing desires. But
Schopenhauer's remedy for "depriving desires their sting" seems to be, as quoted
above, an attainment to "the state of voluntary renunciation, resignation, true
composure and complete will-lessness."

By setting up an either–or scenario between a thoughtless and ongoing affirmation
of the will-to-live and its full denial, Schopenhauer subjects human reality to an
extreme metaphysical dualism. How can complete will-lessness be achieved in
a mortal frame even by a saint? Instead of alluding to moderation, restraint or a
golden mean as thoughtful alternatives to excessive worldliness, Schopenhauer
seems to set up an ideal which is too lofty and too impractical. Also, no methods or
pathways are suggested to achieve this ideal state of "complete will-lessness." In all
these respects, Schopenhauer failed to capture the fuller spirit of either Vedanta or
Buddhism, the two great influences on his theory of the denial of the will-to-live.
The path of *bhakti* (devotional love) as a way out of *maya*, and the essence of the

Buddhist eightfold path, namely, the pathway to *karuna* (compassion), seem to be missing in his treatment of asceticism. But reasons for this rigid dualism and less than adequate treatment of Indian thought are not hard to guess. Schopenhauer is after all a metaphysician with an ambition to explain "everything" neatly and lucidly in a well-crafted system of concepts. That he did not know everything of Indian philosophy can be explained on the basis of the paucity of eastern texts, translations and commentaries in his day and age. Whereas his adoption of Indian concepts is both original and creative and therefore praiseworthy, it will be too much to expect his trans-cultural experiments to be entirely comprehensive and correct. We will discuss Schopenhauer's connection with Vedanta and Buddhism in more detail in a later chapter.

Schopenhauer admits that an authentic denial of the will is both difficult and rare:

> The allurements of hope, the flattery of the present, the sweetness of pleasures, the well-being that falls to the lot of our person amid the lamentations of a suffering world governed by chance and error, all these draw us back to it, and rivet the bonds anew. Therefore Jesus says: It is easier for a camel to go through the eye of a needle, than for a rich man to enter into the kingdom of God. [*W*, I, 380]

But one who is resolved to deny the will embraces "asceticism" with full conviction. He is not merely virtuous. It is no longer sufficient for him to love others like himself:

> But there arises in him a strong aversion to the inner nature whose expression is his own phenomenon, to the will-to-live, the kernel and essence of that world recognized as full of misery ... and his action gives lie to this phenomenon and appears in open contradiction thereto. Essentially nothing but phenomenon of the will, he ceases to will anything, guards against attaching his will to anything, tries to establish firmly in himself the greatest indifference to all things. His body, healthy and strong, expresses the sexual impulse through the genitals, but he denies the will, and gives lie to the body; he desires no sexual satisfaction on any condition. Voluntary and complete chastity is the first stop in asceticism or the denial of the will-to-live. [*W*, I, 380]

It is the aversion to the life of thoughtless willing which resulting in misery, combined with a realization of the unsatisfactoriness of existence as such, that leads a person to resolve to live a life of renunciation, that is, to practice saying no to the will-to-live. The austere life of such a person involves not only "voluntary and complete chastity," but also "voluntary and intentional poverty"; this poverty is not just a matter of giving away one's property to the needy, but this voluntary poverty "is to serve as a constant mortification of the will, so that satisfaction of desires, the sweets of life, may not again stir the will, of which self-knowledge has conceived a horror" (*W*, I, 382). Furthermore, a true denier of the will-to-live gives up self-love altogether and endures "ignominy and suffering with inexhaustible patience and gentleness, returns good for all evil without ostentation, and allows the fire of anger to rise again within him as little as he does the fire of desires" (*W*, I, 382). Schopenhauer intermingles the Hindu myth of reincarnation and the belief that a true *moksha* (salvation) awaits a perfect practitioner of *dharma* (religious life), for whom there is no more rebirth in *samsara*, with his own secular philosophy of will-lessness:

> Finally, if death comes, which breaks up the phenomenon of this will, the essence of such will having long expired through free denial of itself ... then it is most welcome, and is cheerfully accepted as a longed for deliverance. It is not merely the phenomenon ... that comes to an end with death, but the inner being itself that is abolished ... For him who ends thus, the world has at the same time ended. [*W*, I, 382]

The pursuit of salvation from the will-to-live is not just a moral program, but a contemplative and ascetic living which denies the mundane and common life of the flesh. That such denial of will is desirable and possible is visible in the lives of saints and ascetics of Christianity, Hinduism and Buddhism. What went on in their exemplary lives was nothing other and shorter than the denial of the will. Schopenhauer gives us pen portraits of some such lives, first, to underscore that his description of human condition in terms of affirmation and denial of will is neither fantastic nor newly invented by himself but is an age-old world-renouncing lived philosophy of the paragons of wisdom in all major religions of the world:

> And what I have described here with feeble tongue, and only in general terms, is not some philosophical fable, invited by myself and only of today. No, it was the enviable life of so many saints and great souls among the Christians, and even more among the Hindus and Buddhists, and also among the believers of other religions. [*W*, I, 383]

Schopenhauer is not only showing his dexterity in combining eastern concepts and eastern wisdom into his own system, but is exploring the boundary between religion and philosophy. Religious thought and practices that most western philosophers steer clear of seem to be of utmost philosophical relevance to Schopenhauer. He sanitizes religious lives of their respective dogmas and expresses that which is common in them, namely, the denial of the world (*samsara*)-oriented existence or what Schopenhauer calls "the will-to-live":

> Thus it may be that the inner nature of holiness, of self-renunciation, of mortification of one's own will, of asceticism, is here for the first time expressed in abstract terms, and free from everything mythical, as denial of the will-to-live ... A saint may be full of the most absurd superstition, or on the other hand may be a philosopher; it is all the same. His conduct alone is the evidence that he is a saint. [*W*, I, 383]

The outer covering of myth, superstition and dogma should not prevent us from perceiving what is philosophically valuable in the field of religion. At one level, both philosophy and religion offer guidelines to authentic living besides offering in their own distinct ways the knowledge of what is (Being, world, phenomena, reality). Furthermore Schopenhauer seems to have the conviction that wisdom is inseparable from the life of wisdom. The study of the lives of the wise will give us clues about what wisdom is. The study of a philosophical life can be a genuine way of philosophizing. Wilhelm Dilthey (1833–1911), who called for *Lebensphilosophie* (Life-Philosophy) to explore the notions of *Lebenswelt* (life-world) and *Erlebnisse* (Lived-experiences), was an avowed student of biography as a method of philosophizing. Dilthey himself wrote philosophical biographies of Schleiermacher, Hegel and other idealist thinkers. In his *Nature of Philosophy* (1907), he remarks almost in a Schopenhauerian fashion:

> Religious experience would be empty and insipid unless experience of the misery, the depravity or at least the pettiness of human affairs (and the separation and suffering in them), led up to a more holy life far from this circle of perdition. Buddha, Lao-tse and as several pages from the gospel reveal, Christ, have trodden this journey into loneliness; so have Augustine and Pascal. This personal knowledge of life, together with scholarship and traditional customs forms the true basis of philosophy. The personal element in the greatest philosophers rests on this knowledge. Its purification and justification form an essential, indeed the most effective, part of the philosophical systems.[5]

Dilthey believed that autobiography, biography and historiography form a stem from which *Geistwissenschaften* (human studies) branch out. In any case, these are the most important sources for philosophy of life and philosophy as such: "Philosophy must seek its inner coherence not in the world but in man. To understand life as it is lived by man is the will of contemporary man."[6] Dilthey seems to be influenced by Schopenhauer. For Schopenhauer called for the use of biographical studies for philosophizing as well as showing a remarkable openness towards wisdom within the world religions, in addition to using the classical and literary texts, all within his philosophical program. That is why Dilthey remarks that "the mixed style of Schopenhauer, Mommsen and Nietzsche impresses us more than the pathos of Fichte and Schiller."[7]

Schopenhauer foresees that his references to asceticism and his unprecedented experiments with the common ground of philosophy and religion will not only be looked at with derision but that he will be taken to task for not living up to his own notions of renunciation. Here is his reply to his critics:

> It is … just as little necessary for the saint to be a philosopher as for the philosopher to be a saint; just as it is not necessary for a perfectly beautiful person to be a great sculptor, or for a great sculptor to be himself a beautiful person. In general, it is a strange demand on a moralist that he should commend no other virtue than that he himself possesses. [*W*, I, 383]

Although religion does not usually serve as a source for philosophy, denial of the will-to-live can be better understood through a study of the biographies of saints and mystics from all major religious traditions. Schopenhauer finds exemplary

---

5   "The Nature of Philosophy," Vol. V, in H.P. Rickman (ed. and trans.), *W. Dilthey: Selected Writings* (Cambridge: Cambridge University Press, 1976), p. 127.

6   "The Types of World-View," in ibid., p. 135.

7   "Present-day Culture and Philosophy," in ibid., p. 110.

descriptions of the lives of the world-renouncers from both Indian and Christian traditions: "Indian literature, as we see from the little that is so far known to us through translations, is very rich in description of the lives of saints, penitents, *samanas, sanyasis*, and so on ... Among Christians there is also no lack of examples affording us the illustrations that we have in mind" (*W*, I, 384).

After warning us that many such biographies are badly written and full of dogmas of the tradition to which they belong, and after emphasizing the need to sift the essentials from the peripheral details, Schopenhauer recommends some case-studies from the literature available in his times. These include *Mythologie des Indous* by Madame de Polier, *Leben heiliger Seelen* by Tersteegen, *Geschichte der Wiedergeborenen* by Reiz, and especially the Life of St. Francis of Assisi, "that true personification of asceticism and prototype of all mendicant friars". Other favorites of Schopenhauer are listed in *Eastern Monachism* by Spence Hardy which describes the lives of Buddhist monks, and most notably the autobiography of Madame de Guyon, "that great and beautiful soul, whose remembrance always fills me with reverence." The biography of Spinoza, and life-sketches of Fraulein Klettenberg and St. Philip Neri composed by Goethe are also strongly recommended.

Schopenhauer points out that it is no surprise that the history of the world is often silent about the remarkable achievements of those who renounce and overcome the world. For history records for the most part not denial but affirmation of the will-to-live, bringing before the reader "now the superior strength of the individual through his shrewdness, now the might of the many through their mass, now the ascendancy of chance personified as fate, always the vanity and futility of whole striving and effort" (*W*, I, 385):

> The greatest, the most important, and the most significant phenomenon that the world can show is not the conqueror of the world but the overcomer of the world ... The freedom of [the] will first appears in him alone, and by it his actions, now become the very opposite of the ordinary. For the philosophy, therefore ... those accounts of the lives of the saintly, self-denying persons, badly written as they generally are, and mixed up with superstition and nonsense, are ... incomparably more instructive and important than even Plutarch and Livy. [*W*, I, 386]

In other words, if we truly recognize death-contemplation being at the heart of philosophy, as Socrates and the *Katha Upanishad* classically do, then the lives, not just the words of the death-contemplators, become philosophically interesting. These will not then be dismissed as religious and superstitious stuff but studied carefully, to learn more about that possibility of human existence which is other than the common, matter-of-course subservience to the phenomena of the world (*samsara*). By welcoming death within one's life in this manner, an other-worldly existence within the this-worldly life is made possible and one's contemplative creativity blossoms along with an impeccable and exemplary ethical conduct. Lives of such death-contemplators can be read profitably by all but are of especial interest to philosophers who wish to explore the fundamentals of ethics and the spirit of philosophy from all perspectives.

Schopenhauer also uses these biographies of saints and penitents to assert that his exposition of the possibility of the will's denial is neither exotic nor eccentric but lived philosophy of some superior human beings from all ages and all cultures. These biographies "show how old our view is, however now its philosophical expression may be" (*W*, I, 386). Within Christianity, the writings of the apostles show the first stages of asceticism, later developed by penitents, anchorites and monasticism, reaching its fruition in Christian saints and mystics. Schopenhauer recognizes the special importance of Meister Eckhart in this regard, and remarks that mystics present in full clarity the spirit of the New Testament:

> But we find what we call the denial of the will-to-live still further developed, more variously expressed, and more vividly presented in the ancient works in the Sanskrit language than could be the case in the Christian church and the western world. [For] … it was not restricted by an element quite foreign to it, as the Jewish doctrine of faith is in Christianity …
>
> However foreign our knowledge of Hindu literature still is … in the Vedas, Puranas, poetical works, myths, legends of their saints, in aphorisms, maxims and rules of conduct, we see that it ordains love of one's neighbour with complete denial of all self-love; love in general, not limited to the human race but, embracing all that lives …
>
> That which has remained in practice for so long in a nation embracing so many millions, while it imposes the heaviest sacrifices, cannot be an arbitrarily invented freak, but must have its foundation in the very nature of mankind. But besides this we cannot sufficiently wonder at the harmony we find, when we read the life of a Christian penitent or saint and that of India. In spite of such fundamentally different dogmas, customs and circumstances, the endeavour and the inner life of both are absolutely the same. [*W*, I, 387–9]

Thus, according to Schopenhauer, the sublime human possibility of the denial of the will-to-live is exemplified by the saints and mystics of the Christians, Hindu and Buddhist faiths. He finds New Testament Christianity quite close in spirit to and even influenced by Hinduism. Old Testament Christianity, Judaism and Islam, he finds quite discordant with his favourite religions, for they are more this-worldly rather than other-worldly. Thus he carefully chooses his examples of will's denial from later Christianity, Hinduism and Buddhism. The life of one who lives the denial of will is blessed, for it has forever what true experience of art gives us for a few moments:

> How blessed must be the life of a man whose will is silenced not from a few moments, as in the enjoyment of the beautiful, but forever, indeed completely extinguished, except for the last glimmering spark that maintains the body and is extinguished with it … Nothing can distress or alarm him anymore; nothing can any longer move him; for he has cut all the thousand threads of willing which hold us bound to the world, and which as craving, fear, envy and anger drag us here and there in constant pain. [*W*, I, 390]

That such denial is nothing but what we have called "death-contemplation" is evident in the concluding words of the autobiography of Madame de Guyon, the "holy penitent" for whom Schopenhauer has the greatest reverence:

Everything is indifferent to me; I cannot will anything more; often I do not know whether I exist or not … The noonday of glory; a day no longer followed by night; a life that no longer fears death, even in death itself, because death has overcome death, and because whoever has suffered the first death will no longer feel the second. [*W*, I, 391]

Schopenhauer's comparison of Christian and Hindu mysticism is validated by the following quote from the works of the Hindu saint Kabir, a well-known figure in the Hindu *bhakti* movement, whose words echo those of Madame de Guyon:

Kabir, the worldlings die as they must
But hardly anyone knows how to die
One ought to die in such a way
That there is no more dying again in store.[8]

Whereas some rare individuals embark on the path of denial by reflection, that is, by seeing through the *principium individuationis*, there are others, says Schopenhauer, who arrive on it through a colossal personal suffering:

It is the gleam of silver that suddenly appears from the purifying flame of suffering, the gleam of the denial of the will-to-live, of salvation. Occasionally we see even those who were very wicked purified to this degree by the deepest grief and sorrow; they have become different and are completely converted. [*W*, I, 393]

Hence the abiding interest that Schopenhauer shows in his writings to record the crime reports from his favourite English newspapers such as *The Times*, and the various gallows-sermons of those converted on death row. But not just the criminals sentenced to death attain to "the knowledge of the contradiction of the will-to-live with itself": men of great passion too have undergone such a conversion, due to a terrible experience of the misery of life. Schopenhauer mentions the lot of Raymond Lull, who witnessed the cancer-eaten bosom of his long-wooed beloved. In Volume II of *WWR*, he relates the conversion of the Abbé de Rance who happened to kick, in the dark, the severed head of his lady love. This Rance re-established in France, that "cheerful, merry, gay, sensual and frivolous" nation, the Trappist Order which is by far the strictest and longest lasting of all monastic cults. Schopenhauer concludes his description of the sublime but obviously extreme possibility of human existence, which is at the same time, the summit of human knowledge:

It follows from all that has been said, that the denial of the will-to-live, which is the same as what is called complete resignation or holiness, always proceeds from that quieter of the will; and this is the knowledge of its inner conflict and its essential vanity, expressing themselves in the suffering of all that lives … True salvation, deliverance from life and suffering, cannot even be imagined without complete denial of the will. [*W*, I, 397]

---

8   Kabir, *Saloka* 29 in *Adi Granth*; translation mine.

Suicide vs. the Denial

The acceptance of death in one's life is a course that is widely misunderstood. The accusation of suicide was laid even on Socrates, for he chose to drink the cup of hemlock instead of fleeing the custody of the fools. That the rehearsal for death that is philosophy is neither a morose existence, nor a longing for speedy death, had to be clarified by Plato in the *Phaedo*. Although the contemplative life amounts to a voluntary forsaking of what the worldly-minded call "the good life," death-contemplation does not mean opting for the end of life. It is a modified life or authentic life that explores the supreme human possibility of freedom and salvation. To dismiss it as a suicidal attitude is a gross belittling and underestimation of freedom and salvation as real and meaningful goals of human existence.

Thus Schopenhauer, like Socrates, Buddha and a host of classical philosophers before him, had to clarify that the contemplative denial of the will, the life of renunciation is neither morbid subsistence nor comparable to suicide. He had to explain the meaning of the act of suicide in the vocabulary of the will-to-live and re-expose the denial of the will as entirely distinct from the suicidal instinct. In Section 69, Schopenhauer discusses this important issue of the denial vs. suicide and states at the outset that "far from being the denial of the will, suicide is a phenomenon of will's strong affirmation" (*W*, I, 398). The denial is a voluntary renouncing of the pleasures of life whereas suicide is an escape from life's sorrows. The suicide wills life but resents its conditions, or the way it has affected the individual. Schopenhauer explains that the giving-up of life and giving-up of the will-to-live are not the same. Ending life altogether is not the same thing as resolving to live differently and without subservience to the world.

Schopenhauer maintains that the person who takes his own life destroys the phenomenon of the will, not the will itself. Frustrated by the circumstances that blocked his own affirmations of the will and consequent great sorrow, the individual capitulates before the will. This is unlike the life of denial, which confronts and overcomes the will. In case of suicide, the will finds itself so hampered in its advances, that it opts for its typical indifference for the individual phenomenon. Since life is forever assured to the will, which is why it is called "will-to-live," it gives no importance to its individual phenomena: "For that same firm, inner assurance, which enables all of us to live without the constant dread of death, the assurance that the will can never lack its phenomenon, supports the deed even in case of suicide" (*W*, I, 399).

It is here that Schopenhauer gives a simplistic and thoughtless description of the Hindu trinity, maintaining that Shiva represents suicide, Vishnu, self-preservation and Brahma, procreation. This is an example of how Schopenhauer sometimes, perhaps, inadvertently abuses Indian concepts to elucidate his assertions: "As the individual thing is related to the Idea, so is suicide to the denial of the will. The suicide denies merely the individual, not the species" (*W*, I, 399). Thus suicide is a reaction to individual or one's own sufferings, whereas the denial comes from a realization of the inherent and possible sufferings of all who draw their breath. This,

Schopenhauer explained in the beginning of his discussion of the denial of the will-to-live. Suicide is also called the "masterpiece of Maya," since it is "the most blatant expression of the contradiction of the will-to-live with itself." We may conclude that whereas the denial is a free denial of itself based on the knowledge of itself, a distinct possibility in its human phenomenon only, suicide is will's "blatant expression" or "self-contradiction" of another kind. It is not based on will's knowledge of itself but a rash reaction prompted by will's frustration in not realizing its ongoing desires and cravings. In the will's highest form, that is, human existence, the conflict caused by will's commands not only makes the individuals to be willing to exterminate each other but could also prompt "an individual to declare war on himself":

> Suicide is like a sick man who after the beginning of a painful operation that could completely cure him, will not allow it to be completed by prefers to retain his illness ... This is the reason why almost all ethical systems, philosophical as well as religious condemn suicide, though they themselves cannot state anything but strange and sophistical arguments for so doing. [*W*, I, 399]

Will-to-live is not a stuff that can be broken by force: "The will-to-live cannot be abolished by anything except knowledge. Therefore the only path to salvation is that will should appear freely and without hindrance, in order that it can recognize or know its own inner nature in this phenomenon" (*W*, I, 400). This means that suicide obviously involves violence, whereas the denial is the path of non-violence rooted in a superior and fundamental knowledge.

Schopenhauer makes allowance for a special kind of suicide, which can be complementary to the denial of the will-to-live: "This is voluntarily chosen death by starvation at the highest degree of asceticism ... This kind of suicide is so far from being the result of the will-to-live, that such a completely resigned ascetic ceases to live merely because he has ceased to will" (*W*, I, 401). Schopenhauer cites various sources (books and journals) in which accounts of such ascetical suicide can be found. The ancient Indian religion of Jainism contains a tradition followed by its highest monks, according to which death by starvation was practiced. This is, however, an occasional undertaking reserved only for the Jain monks, who have attained to the highest degree of asceticism, and not recommended for or practised by the ordinary faithful.

True Christianity, Denial and Nothingness

The knowledge that is requisite for the denial of the will-to-live must be independent of anything like free choice; "That denial of willing, that entrance into freedom, is not to be forcibly arrived at by intention or design, but comes from the innermost relation of knowing and willing in man" (*W*, I, 404). This fundamental change in one's inner nature is not a matter of intention, design, or deliberate choice, but "comes suddenly, as if flying from without. Therefore the church calls it the effect of grace." In Section 70, Schopenhauer examines the relevant Christian concepts like grace, being born again, original sin, and so on. Not only that, he finds his own philosophy, especially its final moments as described in Book IV of the *WWR*, in accord with the spirit of Christianity, but showing an impact of Hindu thought on his peculiar version of Christianity. Although the concept of God is conspicuous by its absence, his own concepts seem to be secularized versions of some important Christian concepts: "The doctrine of original sin (affirmation of the will) and of salvation (denial of the will) is really the great truth which constitutes the kernel of Christianity, while the rest is in the main only clothing and covering, or something accessory." Schopenhauer has a special fascination for the doctrine of the original sin, which he finds in accord with the Hindu and Buddhist theory of karma. The connection between *karma* (action) and *jnana* (knowledge) is again visible in the following "Christian" interpretation of the will's denial: "Thus we see that genuine virtue and saintliness of disposition have their first origin not in deliberate free choice (works) but in knowledge (faith), precisely as we developed it" (*W*, I, 407). Schopenhauer shows a remarkable ability to draw the insights and concepts from the realm of religion, and modify them for philosophical purposes. He often acts like ancient eastern philosophers who do not demarcate too strictly the respective scopes of philosophy and religion and recognizes that both philosophy and religion ought to offer guidelines for higher living. Without blurring the distinction between philosophy and religion, Schopenhauer illustrates that the range of philosophy extends over the achievements of all human sciences, arts, religions, cultures, from which it can and should draw some of its material but treat it logically, systematically and above all else, "philosophically." It is Schopenhauer's aim to show that his fundamental insights are neither new nor outlandish but perfectly in accord with the grounding principles of both the western and eastern heritages, Christianity and Hinduism alike. His world-view is the philosophical and secular version of the fundamental religious dogmas of east and west:

> Here I have introduced these dogmas of Christian theology, in themselves foreign to philosophy, merely in order to show that the ethics which results from the whole of our discussion ... although possibly new and unprecedented ... is by no means so in its essence ... This system of ethics fully agrees with the Christian dogmas proper ... It is also just as much in agreement with the doctrines and ethical precepts of the sacred books of India, which again are presented in quite different forms. [*W*, I, 408]

Toward the end of his exposition of the denial of the will-to-live, Schopenhauer comments on the charge of "nothingness" that might be ascribed to such denial. The dismissal of holiness, saintliness and salvation, through a simplistic accusation of "nothingness," shows nothing but the common view that reality is nothing more than the worldliness of subjects and objects:

> That we abhor nothingness so much is simply another way of saying that we will live so much, that we are nothing but his will and know nothing but it alone.
> [But] by contemplating the life and the conduct of the saints, to meet with whom is of course rarely granted to us ... but who are brought to our notice by their recorded history

...we have to banish the dark impression of that nothingness, which as the final goal hovers behind all virtue and holiness.

We freely acknowledge that what remains after the complete abolition of the will is, for all who are still full of the will, assuredly nothing. But also conversely, to those in whom the will has turned and denied itself, this very real world of ours with all its suns and galaxies is – nothing. [Footnote: "This is also the *Prajna-paramita* of the Buddhists, the 'beyond all knowledge' ... where subject and object no longer exist."] [*W*, I, 412]

Chapter 4

Schopenhauer and Indian Thought

Schopenhauer was certainly a pioneer in trans-cultural philosophy. A trans-cultural thinker is one who not only compares and contrasts the ideas and concepts of different philosophical traditions but treats a chosen foreign tradition as his own, makes it his own by employing its concepts within his own philosophical projects and problematics. Such a thinker shows the ability to transplant philosophical concepts within two or more traditions in a creative and thoughtful manner, thus treating world philosophy as one body of knowledge.

Philosophies of India, particularly Vedanta and Buddhism, were Schopenhauer's favourite sources for composing and revalidating the universality of his own system. He admired greatly the philosophies and religions of India and cited extensively from their texts, which were beginning to be known in Europe in his times. By the time he published the first edition of *The World as Will and Representation* (*WWR*) in 1819, Schopenhauer was already familiar with Indian thought and cited from it in his *magnum opus*. Two subsequent enlarged editions (1844, 1859) contain even more references to Vedanta and Buddhism. He continues to adopt and creatively employ Indian concepts as part of his philosophical system in his later works, most notably in *On the Will in Nature* (1854) and *Parerga and Paralipomena* (1851).

The issue of Schopenhauer's connections with Indian thought is very crucial for a proper understanding of his philosophy in general and his philosophy concerning death in particular. The following are some of the major problems that need to be resolved:

(a) What precisely is the relation between Schopenhauer's philosophy and Indian thought? Did he know the fundamentals of Vedanta and Buddhism prior to the publication of the first edition of *WWR*, so that we can regard these systems to have decisively influenced his own system?

(b) If Schopenhauer's reading of Indian texts in translation and their available secondary literature grew steadily throughout his career, then is it true that his citations and references grew in direct proportion to his advanced studies of the eastern texts?

(c) Was Schopenhauer's interpretation of Vedantic and Buddhist texts fair as well as comprehensive, even for his day and age? Did he, in any way, misuse Indian concepts to subserve his own system?

(d) Is the relation between Schopenhauer's philosophy and eastern thought properly recognized and properly elucidated in the secondary literature?

In the following pages we will deal with problems such as these in recognizing Schopenhauer's preoccupation with eastern thought. Our discussion of the above mentioned issues and of the central concepts of the Vedanta and Buddhist tradition may seem to be a general analysis. But this appraisal is very much relevant and of vital importance for the problem of death-contemplation in Schopenhauer's thought.

Whether Schopenhauer freely adopted the Indian concepts in his supplementary and later writings, or found in them a re-authentication of his already developed notions of the will-to-live and its denial, one thing is certain. No other western philosopher has studied, elucidated and adopted eastern, especially Indian, philosophies as rigorously as he did. To be so appreciative of a foreign tradition, to treat the philosophies of the world as one, was a remarkably bold step especially in his day and age, when eastern philosophies were still barely known and inadequately translated.

Some General Studies of Schopenhauer and Indian Thought

A question is bound to arise in our minds. Was Schopenhauer's comprehension and use of eastern concepts fair, rigorous and valid, or was it a merely an exotic ornamentation of his own system, for the elaboration of which the eastern concepts were simply pressed into service? The nagging question of pessimism will also arise. Do Vedanta and Buddhism really support the tendencies of pessimism and extreme asceticism that Schopenhauer's philosophy seems to authenticate? Was Schopenhauer's knowledge of eastern philosophy good enough even for his age? Some of these and similar questions are posed by Wilhelm Halbfass in his scholarly work, *India and Europe*.[1]

Halbfass' assessment of Schopenhauer's connections with Indian thought points out that this matter cannot be dealt with simplistically. It will not be fair to simply equate the will-to-live to one of the several Indian concepts such as *maya*, *brahman*, *trisna*, or *upadana*: "How his knowledge of the Indian material was related to the genesis of Schopenhauer's own system is a question which cannot be answered with complete clarity and certainty; his own explicit remarks, in any case, do not provide a sufficient basis for answering it."[2] What Halbfass is referring to is Schopenhauer's own frustration in finding an equivalent Indian concept to his all-important will-to-live and his many declarations concerning the originality of his own system *vis-à-vis* Vedanta and Buddhism. Some of these statements quoted by Halbfass are as follows:

---

1   Wilhelm Halbfass, *India and Europe: An Essay in Understanding* (Albany: State University of New York Press, 1988).

2   Ibid., p. 107.

On the whole, the harmony [of Buddhism] with my teachings is wonderful, all the more so because I wrote the first volume [of *WWR*] between 1814 and 1818 and did not nor could not, have known all that [Briefe, Deussen XV, 470].

By the way, I admit that I do not believe that my doctrine could have ever been formulated before the Upanishads, Plato and Kant were able to cast their light simultaneously onto a human mind.[3]

Halbfass also points out that Schopenhauer alternatively considered the concept of *maya* as equivalent to his notion of *principium individuationis* (*W*, I, 378; *W*, II, 160), and expressed the belief that the Vedantic notion of *brahman* corresponded with his own theory of cosmic will, for it meant "force, will, wish and the propulsive power of creation" [Briefe, Deussen, XV, 522, 563]. "Schopenhauer's basic position was in general, the sages of all times have always said the same [*PPI*, Deussen IV, 348] … Buddha, Eckhardt and I all teach essentially the same [*HN*, Deussen IX, 89]." Halbfass also points out that Schopenhauer saw the Buddhist concept of *upadana* (that is, attachment to the world and worldly objects) as an equivalent of his will-to-live [Briefe II, Deussen, XV, 46].[4]

If we take into account the simplistic equivalence of will-to-live to the concepts such as *brahman, atman, maya, trisna, upadana,* and so on, by Schopenhauer's interpreters, the matter becomes even more complex. However, we cannot ignore the fact that the will-to-live was not propounded primarily for the purposes of comparative philosophy. Halbfass seems to have hit the nail on the head in his concluding remarks:

Schopenhauer's doctrine of the will (primarily) implies a critique of the European tradition of representational and rational thinking, of calculation and planning, science and technology which foreshadows more recent developments … he continued a radical critique of some of the most fundamental pre-suppositions of the Judeo-Christian tradition such as the notion of a personal God, the uniqueness of the human individual and the meaning of history as well as the modern western belief in the power of the intellect, rationality, planning and progress.[5]

This means that while Indian concepts did cast a spell on Schopenhauer's thinking, he did not simply borrow them to build his own system. The concept of the will-to-live was primarily enunciated to critique and correct the fundamental Judeo-Christian and western metaphysical assumptions that had taken both Christian religion and western philosophy in its grip; Hegel's system being one example of a full adoption of these assumptions. The will-to-live indeed corrects the all entrenched western assumptions concerning the idea of a personal God, the supremacy of the rational and the dismissal of the instinct. The Indian concepts are alluded to by Schopenhauer to elucidate not only the inner nature of the will-to-live but also exemplify how an

---

3 Ibid.
4 Ibid., pp. 111, 112, 119.
5 Ibid., p. 120.

authentic denial and overcoming of it is possible and deemed desirable by the saintly thinkers of all world traditions of noble religions and philosophies.

Indeed, the Vedic notions of *maya*, *mamta* (mine-ness) and *moha* (passionate love), *aham* (ego) all illustrate the nature of will-to-live and so do the Buddhist notions of *trisna* (craving) and *upadana* (attachment). However, it would be most objectionable to equate the will-to-live with the Vedantic notion of *brahman*. This notion of divine Being seems to have hardly anything in common with the blind, irrational urge to live and live it up, as conceived by Schopenhauer. As we shall elaborate in the next section, the concept of the denial of the will-to-live touches a degree of metaphysical dualism and extreme asceticism combined with a pessimistic dismissal of *samsara* that Vedanta and Buddhism do not advocate.

There are some other published accounts of Schopenhauer's connection with Indian philosophy which are not as well balanced as Halbfass' but interesting and valuable for other reasons. Moira Nicholls, in her article "The Influences of Eastern Thought on Schopenhauer's Doctrine of the Thing-in-itself,"[6] offers useful information about Schopenhauer's citations of eastern thought in his works, even though her thesis about shifts in Schopenhauer's doctrines after 1818 is flawed and unconvincing. The following factual information is noteworthy.

> Volume I of *WWR* (1819) contains about eight references to Buddhist thought, five of which are added in later editions (1844) and (1859) of that volume. By comparison, in Volume II, first published in 1844 (when a second edition of Volume I was also published), there are at least thirty references to Buddhism. References to Hindu thought in Volume I number over fifty, seven of which are added in the later editions, and in Volume II, there are over forty-five references to Hinduism. While these figures are only approximate, they indicate a marked rise in Schopenhauer's knowledge of and interest in Buddhist thought from 1818 on, and a strong and consistent interest in Hindu thought from 1813 until his death in 1860. That Schopenhauer was in the habit of adding references to his earlier works is clear from the following footnoted comment in the 1859 edition of the first volume: 'In the last forty years Indian literature has grown so much in Europe that if I now wished to complete this note to the first edition, it would fill several pages' (*W*, I, 388 n). Such comments indicate that Schopenhauer had an abiding interest in eastern philosophy, and that he was keen to demonstrate parallels between his own doctrines and those of the East.[7]

So far all of Nicholls' assertions are acceptable. We should keep in mind, however, that statistical analysis can only provide us with part of the truth and can very easily lead us astray. Moira Nicholls' thesis, based on meticulously presented statistical data, remains seriously flawed due to reasons to be outlined below. The following conclusions of Nicholls are enough to make Schopenhauer turn in his grave:

---

6   Moira Nicholls, "The Influences of Eastern Thought on Schopenhauer's Doctrine of the Thing-in-itself," in C. Janaway (ed.), *The Cambridge Companion to Schopenhauer* (Cambridge: Cambridge University Press, 1999).

7   Ibid., p. 177.

Three identifiable shifts in Schopenhauer's doctrine of the thing-in-itself occur between the publication of the first volume of *WWR* in 1818 and his later works. The first shift concerns the knowability of the thing-in-itself, the second ... [its] nature, the third ... his explicit attempt to assimilate his own doctrine ... with eastern doctrines. Schopenhauer asserts numerous times throughout his works that the thing-in-itself is will or will-to-live and he claims that we know this through direct intuition in self-consciousness ...

However ... in his later works ... he seems to withdraw the claim that in self-consciousness we are aware of the will, suggesting instead that in self-consciousness we are aware no more than our phenomenal willings ...

The second shift ... [occurs when he] introduces the idea that thing-in-itself has multiple aspects, only one of which is will. In other aspects are the objects of awareness of such persons as mystics, saints and ascetics, who have denied the will ...

[Regarding] [t]he third shift ... I have identified six passages in which Schopenhauer asserts that the thing-in-itself can be described as will, but only in a metaphorical sense ... [thus] similar views expressed in eastern thought ... .[8]

In response to Nicholls' interpretations it might be said at the outset that there are no shifts in Schopenhauer's doctrine of the thing-in-itself, for which Schopenhauer's advanced readings of eastern thought, or anything else is responsible. Nothing is clearer than the fact that Being of all beings is named will-to-live by Schopenhauer. This thing-in-itself (a Kantian term) was never claimed to be either entirely absent or entirely (or precisely) known in human consciousness. If further attempts are made to describe it in conjunction with classical Vedantic and Buddhist notions to spell out what these systems regard as Being of beings, that is, more broadly as *brahman* or *nirvana*, or more specifically as *maya* or *trishna*, this by no means indicate a "shift" in Schopenhauer's doctrine of will. It is well known that despite the dismal sales of the first edition of *WWR*, Schopenhauer regarded it as the ultimate and complete metaphysical system, to which the rest of his works are a series of footnotes. That is why subsequent additions to this work, constituting Volume II, are simply called "supplements," and the chapters of Volume II are written in concordance with the sections of the four books of Volume I. His later works other than *WWR* are also, from his point of view, further elaborations of the original statement of his world-view. Nicholls' assertion that in the later works Schopenhauer "seems to withdraw the claim that in self-consciousness we are aware of the will" amounts to scholarly quibbling. Schopenhauer consistently maintains that for the most part one is not aware of the will being the source of one's wants, desires and urges, but that human beings do have the possibility of knowing the will's machinations, and of denying it, as examples of mystics and ascetics show us. As far as Nicholls' reference to Schopenhauer's later description of the will being possible "only in a metaphorical sense" is concerned, it reads like: coming more and more in contact with eastern mystics' metaphorical understanding of the thing-in-itself, Schopenhauer's own doctrine allowed only a metaphorical account of the will. Nothing of that sort ever happened. Although Schopenhauer made use of the biographical materials from both

---

8   Ibid., p. 171–6.

theistic (Christian, Hindu) and non-theistic (Buddhist, Jain) religious traditions, he did so for philosophical purposes, without losing sight of his own secular metaphysical elucidation of his system. That is why he repeatedly warns the reader in Book 4 of *WWR*, that the religious dogmas and superstitious beliefs of such mystics, saints and ascetics should be disregarded. However, any attempt to define the thing-in-itself in precise terms may not be entirely successful. This difficulty is acknowledged by Schopenhauer in both his early and later works.

Another comprehensive study of Schopenhauer's eastern sources is done by Bhikkhu Nanajivako in his book *Studies in Comparative Philosophy*.[9] Nanajivako, who is a practicing Buddhist monk currently living in Sri Lanka, was born in Yugoslavia. His book provides some useful insights on Schopenhauer's connections with Indian philosophy in general and Buddhism in particular. In Chapter 1, Nanajivako begins with a critique of Euro-centric interpretations of Schopenhauer and demonstrates with numerous citations the central role of Indian thought in this thinker's system. Chapter 2, 3 and 4 are devoted exclusively to Schopenhauer's connections with Buddhist thought and contain several passages attempting to de-emphasize the roots of Schopenhauer's thought in Vedanta. Nanajivako shows his bias against Vedanta in his highly favored treatment of Buddhism in trying to posit the thesis that although Vedic thought within "fragmentary" *Upanishads* was initially a significant influence on Schopenhauer, this thinker in good time grew out of mutually discordant Hindu systems of thought and in his more mature years opted for the more methodical and cohesive Buddhist system (especially, in its orthodox earlier *Theravada* version based in Sri Lanka). Accordingly, in Chapters 2, 3 and 4, Nanajivako, having dismissed Vedanta in Chapter 1, focuses on Schopenhauer's commentaries on Buddhism sprinkled throughout his earlier and later works. In fact, each and every statement of Schopenhauer regarding Buddhism is reproduced in these chapters, making these approximately one hundred pages a useful research tool.

As we will show in our following assessment of Nanajivako's labors, there is no clear evidence that Schopenhauer ever lost his admiration of Vedanta and allied Hindu systems. Nor did he ever show a preference for one over the other with respect to Vedanta and Buddhism. In order to elucidate his own insights and concepts, Schopenhauer cited comparable notions within Vedanta and Buddhism alternatively. For instance in his essay on Death in Volume II (Chapter 41) of *WWR*, he discusses both the Hindu myth of reincarnation and the Buddhist myth of rebirth, affirming in passing that in regard to metempsychosis, "we find this doctrine in its subtlest form, and coming nearest to the truth in Buddhism" (*W*, II, 504). Sporadic observations of this kind should not lead us to conclude that Schopenhauer prefers Buddhism over Vedanta on the whole. For in the same essay he also remarks "the conviction here described and arising directly out of the apprehension of nature must have been extremely lively in those sublime authors of the Upanishads of the Vedas,

---

9   Bhikkhu Nanajivako, *Studies in Comparative Philosophy* (Columbo: Lakehouse Publishers, 1983).

who can scarcely be conceived as mere human beings" (*W*, II, 475). Schopenhauer admires and cites the *Bhagvadgita* (*W*, II, 473) as well as the Buddha (*W*, II, 504, 508) in the same work.

Nanajivako reacts to several "Euro-centric" interpretations of Schopenhauer's thought that abound in the relevant secondary literature, which either de-emphasize or bypass the Indian sources. According to Nanajivako, the importance of Indian thought in Schopenhauer's system is quite visible; "Even the first volume of ... [*WWR*], which appeared in 1819 ... is interspersed from its preface to the last paragraph with quotations from Indian wisdom and reflections on these."[10] By referring to Schwaab's *La Renaissance Orientale*,[11] Nanajivako points out that Schopenhauer, like Goethe and Schelling, had attended Friedrich Maier's lectures in oriental thought. In 1813, Schopenhauer received a copy of the *Oupnekhat* a Latin translation of the *Upanishads* from a Persian version. To re-emphasize that Schopenhauer's preoccupation with Indian thought began quite early in his career, Nanajivako points towards a footnote quotation from the *Oupnekhat* in the early manuscripts (p. 106, sec. 191) dated 1914, five years before *WWR* was first published.[12] In sec. 192 (p. 107), there is this: "The wiser Indians started from the subject, from *atman, jivatma* ... ." In the same year (sec. 213, p. 120) the first mention is made of *maya*; in the next reference (sec. 214, p. 136) *maya* is defined as "the inward moving force of the corporeal world." In the notes of the following two years, this definition (of *maya*) is further elaborated. These earliest references may suffice to show how deep the first impact of Indian thought was on Schopenhauer at the very time when the idea of his whole system was beginning to germinate in his mind.

Nanajivako is right that Schopenhauer was quite familiar and impressed with the thought contained in the *Upanishads*. That he regarded *Oupnekhat* his prize possession is well known. He will pay the book the ultimate tribute in the following words in *Parerga* and *Paralipomena*. "[It is] the most edifying reading [with the exception of the original text (1851)] that could be possible in this world; it has been the solace of my life and will be the solace of my death" (*PP*, II, sec. 184).

However, Nanajivako's several attempts to prove his subsequent general hypothesis that Schopenhauer somehow grew out of his initial fascination with Vedanta and regarded only Buddhism as the most worthwhile philosophy, fails to convince us. Why would anyone view Schopenhauer as dismissive of Vedic thought in his more mature years, when as late as in 1851 he pays a supreme tribute to the *Oupnekhat*, its subject-matter, and in the words of Halbfass "throughout his life, clung to the belief that this [book] was a definite achievement and key to a philosophical understanding of the Upanishads."[13] The following theses of Nanajivako are unconvincing and misleading.

---

10 Ibid., p. 14.
11 Raymond Schwaab, *La Renaissance Orientale* (Paris: Payot, 1950).
12 Nanajivako, *Studies in Comparative Philosophy*, p. 22.
13 Halbfass, *India and Europe*, p. 106.

At later stages it can be clearly seen how this expansion of the Vedantic idea of *maya* subsided and its world-creating meaning was taken over by the more explicitly Buddhist connotation of *samsara* … In the index to both volumes of the *WWR*, 16 references to the term *maya* are listed from the first volume and only 2 from the second (i.e., 25 years later).

It seems to me that the longest text on Buddhism … from the second edition of the *FRPSR* (1847) … can be taken as a safest landmark … when the transition from a predominantly Vedantic to a prevalently Buddhist orientation was accomplished.[14]

The term *samsara* is a perennial concept of the Indian tradition, rooted in Hindu belief of reincarnation, and older than the Buddhist faith itself. Furthermore, the term *maya* continues to be frequently used in Schopenhauer's later works, and is in no way regarded by him as a synonym or a substitute for the term *samsara*. It is quite logical to assume that Schopenhauer's knowledge of both Vedanta and Buddhism grew alongside the availability of more and more Indian texts and translations in Europe, and through his readings of those new materials he gained new insights and formed occasional preferences of one school over the other with respect to individual philosophical issues. For example, he finds the Buddhist concept of *palingenesis* closer to his own account of the indestructibility of the will beyond an individual's death than the Hindu theory of "metempsychosis". He fully realizes and mentions that the subtleties of *palingenesis* are meant for philosophers only and the masses in both Buddhist and Hindu camps followed similar and simpler beliefs concerning reincarnation. Thus in Schopenhauer's thought there is no such thing as a break with Vedanta and full endorsement of Buddhism on the whole. Obviously, Schopenhauer acquired more comprehensive knowledge of the Indian systems as his reading of the available literature grew. But he continues to treat the eastern and western concepts equally and interchangeably as part of his trans-cultural tendencies in order to expose his own system from various angles. There was no abatement in his admiration and love of the eastern concepts from both Vedanta and Buddhism.

Schopenhauer and his Western Critics

Let us now look at some examples in the secondary literature, of gross misunderstandings and trivializations of some of Schopenhauer's important concepts, these misunderstandings being rooted in a lack of familiarity and sympathy with even the basic concepts of Indian thought. The fundamental assumptions of this thinker, concerning the sufferings and undesirable status of the world, eternal justice, death and salvation, are grounded in his thoughtful, rigorous, creative but sympathetic readings of Vedanta and Buddhism in available translations and commentaries. However, Schopenhauer's modern interpreters, for the most part being innocent of even the basics of Indian thought, have often misunderstood and oversimplified this thinker's fundamental positions on the status of this world, existence, death

---

14 Nanajivako, *Studies in Comparative Philosophy*, p. 17, 23.

and suffering. Although these same interpreters have done a fine job in tracing Schopenhauer's relations with the Platonic and Kantian systems, they are either silent or too brief on Schopenhauer's eastern connections and his trans-cultural experiments. One of the most bewildering aspects of Schopenhauer's thought for many of his western interpreters is his apparent disdain of the world and existence as such. His condemnation of individualism, an all-important western value, as well as his emphasis on suffering and overlooking of happiness, are viewed as equally puzzling. Thus, labels of extreme pessimism, absurdity, perversity and hypocrisy are applied to Schopenhauer's thought by some well-established scholars. Schopenhauer is widely known as a pessimistic thinker and he himself is never shy of rejecting optimistic notions such as those that label our world the best of all possible worlds. He is hard on the so-called optimistic thinkers and systems of all hues. Nevertheless, the current secondary literature often judges him more pessimistic than he is and caricatures both his life and work as odd, eccentric and puzzling. This has happened largely due to a lack of appreciation of Schopenhauer's eastern sources.

Schopenhauer's thought concerning individual existence and the human potential for salvation is the most misunderstood aspect in the secondary literature. The statements such as the following have caused much confusion: "To desire immortality for the individual is to perpetuate an error forever, for at bottom every individuality is really only a special error, a false step, something that it would be better should not be, in fact, something from which it is the real purpose of life to bring us back" (*W*, II, 492).

This is the kind of statement that is so difficult for many Schopenhauer scholars to accept at its face value. They often attribute such convictions of the thinker to his pessimism or begin to see superficial contradictions in his standpoints. For example, Michael Fox in his article "Schopenhauer on Death, Suicide and Self-renunciation" frustratingly remarks:

> The doctrine of *palingenesis* as promulgated by Schopenhauer is indeed difficult to comprehend, and there is more than one lacuna in his account … After all Schopenhauer makes the perverse claim that for mankind it would have been better not to have come into being than to exist; life is merely a disturbing interruption of the blissful non-existence. Schopenhauer's doctrine of self-renunciation must be examined independently of his entirely perverse and absurd position … that man is guilty and inexpungeably sinful, not because of his deeds but merely because he exists.[15]

In a similar unsympathetic reading of Schopenhauer's statement "we are at bottom something that ought not to be" (*W*, II, 507), David Cartwright, in his article "Schopenhauer on Suffering, Death, Guilt and Consolation of Metaphysics," remarks: "We suffer and die because we deserve it. The world is perfectly retributive. We deserve what we receive because we are guilty. We are guilty because we exist.

---

15 Michael Fox, "Schopenhauer on Death, Suicide and Self-renunciation," in Michael Fox (ed.), *Schopenhauer: His Philosophical Achievement* (New York: Barnes and Noble Books, 1980), p. 161.

Schopenhauer's logic is now as clear as it is unconvincing … If we explore these claims they seem highly implausible."[16]

A misunderstanding of Schopenhauer's attitude toward *samsara* consistent with his reading of Vedanta and Buddhism, a failure to distinguish between "excessive worldliness" and "the world," a refusal to take seriously the wisdom behind the myth of reincarnation, a belief of the two-thirds of humanity including that of the ancient Greeks, has driven many contemporary interpreters of Schopenhauer to extreme judgments of not only this man's philosophy but of the man himself. For instance, Bryan Magee in his recent book, *The Philosophy of Schopenhauer*, says:

> In the light of the present day knowledge there can be little doubt that Schopenhauer's despairing view of the world, above all his conviction of the terribleness of existence as such, were in some degree neurotic manifestations which had roots in his relationship with his mother … If actions speak louder than words, his life as he in fact lives it … tells us of a man in whom protean pleasures are being experienced side by side with mountainous frustration, misanthropy and desolate miseries of neurosis. [17]

Although John Atwell also does not incorporate an adequate analysis of eastern thought in his book *Schopenhauer: The Human Character*, while discussing the notion of "eternal justice" he offers an important rejoinder to the name-calling that abounds in secondary literature:

> Now if the doctrine of eternal justice is "absurd" or "perverse", then it is not so in itself, but only because Schopenhauer's entire metaphysical thesis – the world is will – is absurd or perverse; for the doctrine of eternal justice follows with strict necessity from the metaphysical thesis … Consequently, one cannot logically accept the metaphysical thesis or even regard it as plausible or worthwhile or insightful (as critics often suggest) and then reject the doctrine of eternal justice or regard it as nonsense (as the very same critics often do).[18]

Atwell correctly identifies the tendency of selective reading of Schopenhauer in the current secondary literature. We wish to show that the concepts often taken to task or rejected are frequently those that emanate from Schopenhauer's sympathies with the Vedic and Buddhist systems. These fundamental concepts, pre-suppositions and rationales of Schopenhauer are cast aside due to the critics' unfamiliarity (and even unfairness) toward eastern thought.

---

16 David Cartwright, "Schopenhauer on Suffering, Death, Guilt and the consolation of Metaphysics," in Eric von der Luft (ed.), *Schopenhauer: New Essays in Honour of his 200th Birthday* (Lewiston, NY: Edwin Mellon Press, 1988).

17 Bryan Magee, *The Philosophy of Schopenhauer* (Oxford: Clarendon Press, 1997), pp. 13, 260.

18 John E. Atwell, *Schopenhauer: The Human Character* (Philadelphia, PA: Temple University Press, 1990), p. 195.

In response to these half-baked critiques, we must say that there is nothing absurd or perverse about Schopenhauer's deep appreciation of the Vedantic and Buddhist standpoint, that having to be reborn in *samsara* is no event for celebration. The bliss of *nirvana* must be contrasted with the unsatisfactory nature and vulgarity of *samsaric* existence. The need for salvation must be understood as the unsatisfactory status of thoughtless worldliness. The portrayal of *nirvana* as a release from the cycle of rebirth is a mythological exposition of the philosophical standpoint that *samsara* or downright worldliness ought not be valued. Thought and thoughtful life must overcome immoderate worldliness. To desire perpetuation of individuality, to give in to self-love (*mamta*), ego (*aham*) and *moha* (mine-ness), is the same as saying yes to *samsara*, and hence neither desirable nor praiseworthy. Schopenhauer's statement that "at bottom every individuality is a special error, a false step, something that it would be better not to be" is a reiteration of the Vedantic message that to take the ego (*aham*) as real is to dismiss one's larger and real self (*atman*). All individualities and diversities are superficial in contrast to the one-ness of subjects and objects, or the truth of "that thou art" (*tat twam asi*). Agreeing with Vedanta, Schopenhauer maintains that the real purpose of human life is to bring ourselves back from the individuality-based, narrow-minded living that affirms and remains involved in the rational pursuits of the irrational and blind urges of the will-to-live that produce *samsara* for us from moment to moment.

Schopenhauer and Indian Thought: A Critique and Final Assessment

Just as some contemporary western scholars are puzzled about Schopenhauer's forays into eastern thought, some eastern scholars are equally skeptical about this thinker's use and abuse of eastern concepts within his system. Although many eastern scholars, themselves well schooled in western philosophy, do recognize Schopenhauer's preoccupation with Vedanta and Buddhism with admiration and curiosity, they nevertheless remain skeptical about his interpretations. One of the major objections is concerning the issue of pessimism. According to them, it is highly unpardonable to label either Vedanta or Buddhism as pessimistic on the whole. Thus, if Schopenhauer uses these systems and their concepts to revalidate his own pessimistic outlook of the world, it amounts to a misunderstanding and even an abuse of these world-views. Everything rests on a proper, sympathetic and fundamental understanding of the perennial concepts such as *brahman* (Being), *atman* (soul), *maya*, *samsara*, *karma*, reincarnation and rebirth, *nirvana*, *avidya* (ignorance), *trisna* (craving), *karuna* (compassion), *bhakti* (devotion), and so on. The practitioners of Hindu and Buddhist philosophies and religions would resent the other worldliness of their traditions to be interpreted as "pessimistic."

If we take Schopenhauer's word for it, the outline of his basic system as it appears in the first edition of *WWR* (1819) was not composed under the spell of eastern thought. There is evidence, however, that his studies of eastern texts had already begun as early as 1813, as he had started to record his impressions of Vedanta texts in his

Early Manuscripts. After the appearance of *WWR*, Schopenhauer was himself struck by the affinity of his system with the insights of eastern philosophies, as he undertook serious studies of the available eastern literature in European languages. In any case, there should be no doubt that all the works of Schopenhauer subsequent to the first edition of *WWR* show a deeper appreciation of eastern concepts. Schopenhauer's own interpretations of his already complete system, including its supplements in the form of Volume II of *WWR*, and later essays written in the popular format such as those in *Parerga and Paralipomena*, contain numerous references to the eastern philosophies and concepts. In a way, Schopenhauer made a lasting contribution to the popularization, legitimacy and recognition of Indian philosophies in the West, as in the last decade of his life he enjoyed his long-overdue popularity.

It is clear to any serious student of Schopenhauer's work that he maintained a life-long admiration and deep interest in Vedanta. This is evident in his numerous references to the Vedic concepts and doctrines throughout his early and later works. As mentioned above, this does not mean that his perceptive and creative accounts of Vedic thought were always comprehensive as well as valid. Schopenhauer's validations of atheism, asceticism and, above all, pessimism are obviously in discord with the spirit of Vedanta. That is why it will be most objectionable to compare his will-to-live with either *brahman* or *atman*; it may rather be comparable to *maya*. Although *brahman* is described as beyond everything, indifferent and neutral by Sankara, it is also called *sat-chitta-ananda* (everlasting, pure consciousness and blissful) ground of all entities. Thus, atheism and pessimism are ruled out by Vedanta. Hinduism becomes explicitly theistic and devotional with the advent of the *Bhagvadgita* ("the song of the *bhagvat*, or the grand dispenser"). Although Schopenhauer correctly points out the important contributions of ascetic role-models of gurus, saints, *sadhus*, *samanas*, *munis* and *rishis* and their remarkable otherworldly lifestyles within the Hindu tradition, it cannot be taken as an authentication of "asceticism" as recommended by Schopenhauer. For the pursuit of *dharma* is not a simple matter of affirmation and denial in Hinduism. It is not merely a decision to deny or stifle worldliness. The Vedanta tradition includes in itself the method of *bhakti* (devotion, love), which is to be combined (*yoga*) with knowledge (*jnana* and living activity (*karma*) to attain union (*yoga*) with the divine *brahman*. In other words, the method of *bhakti* is not the path of asceticism but an alternative to asceticism, a spontaneous embracing of the other-worldly in this world, an invitation to higher love in this life. The work of the *bhakti* saints that appeared as part of the southern (sixth-century onward) and northern (thirteenth-century onward) *bhakti* movement of Hindu revivalism shows a personal and passionate longing to identify with the object of devotion (*ish*). The role and the superiority of the way of *bhakti* is very succinctly outlined in the following words of the sixteenth-century *bhakti* saint, Eknath (1548–1608):

> Though one restrains the senses, yet they are not restrained. Though one renounces sexual desires, yet they are not renounced. Again and again they return to torment one. For that reason "the flame of *hari-bhakti* was lit by the Veda". There is no need to suppress the

senses; the desire of sensual pleasure ceases of itself. So mighty is the power that lies in *hari-bhakti* ...

The senses that *yogis* suppress *bhaktas* devote to the worship of *bhagvat*, offer to *bhagvat*. Yogis suffer in the flesh ... the followers of *bhakti* become forever emancipated. Though he has no knowledge of the *Vedas*, still by one so ignorant may the real *atman* [self] be apprehended. The condition of *brahman* may easily be attained and possessed ...

Women, *sudras* [the low caste] and all the others ... can be borne by the power of *sraddha* [faith] and *bhakti* to the other shore [of the ocean of *samsara*] ...

Wherever the *bhakta* sets his foot that path is God. Then in every step he takes, his *bhakti* is an offering to *brahman*.[19]

It is obvious that Schopenhauer paid hardly any attention to *bhakti* as an important aspect of Hinduism. But for this he cannot be blamed. There were hardly any accounts of *bhakti* available in the Europe of his times. Only *jnana* (knowledge)-oriented, intellectualized Hinduism was made available in western terminology. *Bhakti*, which is what makes Indian philosophies "living philosophies", that is, guidelines to higher living, is given hardly any importance by scholars of eastern philosophy even today. It is often regarded as a religious method and its importance within philosophy as such has yet to be acknowledged. In any case, *bhakti* as the soul of *prema* (higher love), and its Buddhist counterpart *karuna* (compassion), are mentioned but not properly incorporated in his thought-system by Schopenhauer; otherwise his extreme versions of asceticism, atheism and pessimism would have been mitigated. Thus, in a way, Schopenhauer did abuse Vedic and Buddhist concepts for his own pessimistic purposes, and failed to trace their wider and more moderate interpretations.

Let us now look at Schopenhauer's version of Buddhism. It is easy to be impressed with a narrower and simpler meaning of the all-important term *dukkha* (suffering) that appears in the standard statement of the four noble truths that appears within the various extant manuscripts of different Buddhist schools and sects. In the first sermon of the Buddha, the first noble truth is presented in the following Buddhist scriptural discourse (*sutra*):

Now this, O monks, is the noble truth of *dukkha*: birth is *dukkha*, old age is *dukkha*, sickness is *dukkha*, death is *dukkha*, sorrow, lamentation, dejection and despair are *dukkha*.

---

19 Quoted by Nicol Macnicol, *Indian Theism* (Delhi: Munshilal Manohailal, 1915), p. 270, translation revised by the author. Eknath seems to be convinced that *bhakti* originated in the Vedas, it did not begin with the *Bhagvadgita* but was there in the very origin of Hindu thought. For more descriptions and historical accounts of *bhakti*, see my following articles: "The Pivotal Role of Bhakti in Indian World-views," *Diogenes*, 156 (1991): 65–81; "Bhakti as a Measure of Love and the Vedic Tradition," *Dialogue and Alliance*, 6 (1993): 64–75; "The Ancient Origins of *Bhakti* and the *Dharma* of the Buddha," *Journal of Dharma*, 22 (1997): 460–69; "Bhakti as the Essence and Measure of Art," in G. Marchiano and R. Milani (eds), *Frontiers of Trans-culturality in Contemporary Aesthetics* (Turin: Trauben, 2001), pp. 187–96.

Contact with unpleasant things is *dukkha*, not getting what one wishes is *dukkha*. In short, the five *skandas* of grasping are *dukkha*.[20]

The literal meaning of *dukkha* is sorrow or pain, which is used in various translations of this basic text. The repeated use of the term and its literal meaning create the impression that the Buddha takes a gloomy view of human reality and maintains that all life is suffering. This would justify the reading that both the Buddha and Buddhism are pessimistic and blind to the happiness and glory of human existence. But when we notice and recognize that the Buddha took pains to specify the inevitable occasions of *dukkha* in human existence, and does offer a diagnosis as well as a way out of *dukkha* in the next three noble truths, then we cannot call the whole system as pessimistic. If the Buddha wanted to say that all life is suffering he could have composed the first noble truth in one phrase: "O monks, this life (*jivan*) is dukkha." Instead, he thoughtfully considers the outstanding, inevitable and universal occasions of unsatisfactoriness that pervade human existence.

"Birth (*janama*) is dukkha" is the most radical statement, which by the way, deeply impresses Schopenhauer. It is consistent with the Vedic, pre-Buddhist conviction of the Indian tradition, that coming into *samsara* cannot be deemed as positive even though only the human birth (that is, existence) offers an opportunity for liberation (*moksha* or *nirvana*). Accordingly, Schopenhauer maintains that only in its human form, the will has the possibility to know and deny itself. The Buddha offered an original ontology to the Indian philosophical tradition; an ontology quite different from that of Vedanta, but he refrained from being too original. He had to retain in his system the myth of reincarnation, albeit in its modified version which Schopenhauer calls "*Palingenesis,*" and keep intact the theory of *karma*. Both the belief in rebirth until nirvana, and the accumulation of *karma* fit very well within the theory of dependent origination, another hallmark of Buddhism. Thus, "birth is *dukkha*" means thoughtless preoccupation with *samsara* is unsatisfactory, almost demeaning to human existence. It is something comparable to Socrates' statement that it is not living that counts but living well. Being born in *samsara* and being subject to it, itself cannot be called a happy event, for the real purpose of life is to gain salvation from *samsara*. It is for a good reason that the Buddha begins his catalogue of *dukkha* with a mythological statement in the first noble truth which is otherwise exceedingly logical. Hence, it would be simplistic to regard Buddhism either pessimistic or a justification of pessimism due to the way it presents its noble truth of *dukkha*. Notice that "sorrow" itself is named as one of the occasions of *dukkha*. Dukkha must be understood in the larger sense of "unsatisfactoriness": "In short, the five *skandhas* are dukkha" means that dukkha is so pervasive that all the five aggregates of attachment, of which the human entity is composed (that is, form, sensation, perception, pre-dispositions and consciousness) can be the recipients of

---

20 From *Samyutta-nikaya*, in Radhakrishnan S. and Moore, C.A. (eds), *A Sourcebook of Indian Philosophy* (Princeton, NJ: Princeton University Press, 1973), p. 274.

dukkha. Schopenhauer refers to the four noble truths as follows in Volume II of *WWR*:

> In [Buddhism] all improvement, conversion and salvation to be hoped from this world of suffering, from this *samsara* proceed from knowledge of the four fundamental truths: (1) *dolor* (suffering) (2) *doloris ortus* (origin of suffering) (3) *dolaris interitus* (cessation of suffering), (4) *octopartita* via *ad doloris sedationem* (the eightfold path to the calming of suffering) … The explanation of these four truths is found in *Burnouf*, p. 629 and in all descriptions of Buddhism.
>
> Christianity belongs to the ancient true, and sublime faith of mankind. This faith stands in contrast to the false, shallow and pernicious optimism that manifest itself in Greek paganism, Judaism, and Islam. [*W*, II, 623]

Thus, Schopenhauer admires Buddhism because of its supposed pessimism and regards genuine Christianity and Hinduism equally pessimistic as opposed to the pernicious optimism that raises its head in paganism, the Old Testament and Islam. In the above quoted statement Schopenhauer clearly oversimplifies the first truth by describing its essence in one word, that is, suffering, and by de-emphasizing the insight of the next three truths. The second noble truth is:

> Now this, O monks, is the noble truth of the cause of *dukkha*: that craving (*tanha*) which leads to rebirth, combined with pleasure and lust, finding pleasure here and there, namely the craving for passion, the craving for existence, the craving for non-existence.

Tanha or *trishna* is identified as the cause of *dukkha*. This *trishna* is named as one "which leads to rebirth." *Logos* and *mythos* are again combined to identify *trishna* as the cause of *dukkha* and the cause of rebirth, that reaffirms that rebirth is not the goal of the wise, *nirvana* is. Manifesting itself in pleasures and lusts, this *trishna* is of three kinds, that is, craving for passion, for continued existence and, oddly enough, craving can take the form of an obsessive desire for *nirvana*. This craving for *nirvana* is self-defeating, as it is said in *visuddhi-magga*: "Nirvana is but not the man who seeks it, the path exists but not the traveler on it."[21] It is interesting to note that *trishna* comes closest to Schopenhauer's notion of the will-to-live, for it too is the cause of *dukkha*, as well as rebirth, being indestructible in the species. It is at the bottom of all pleasure-seeking and lusts, the one that ties us to our dear lives. That is why the will-to-live is called a "pleonasm" by Schopenhauer, for will and life go hand in hand. The third noble truth offering the possibility of the complete removal of *dukkha* can only be called "optimistic":

> Now this, O monks, is the noble truth of the cessation of *dukkha*: the cessation without a remainder of that craving, abandonment, forsaking, release, non-attachment.

The third truth assures us that the cessation of craving "without a remainder" is a human possibility. It is not fantastic to obtain the release. Non-attachment is

---

21 Radhakrishnan and Moore, *A Sourcebook of Indian Philosophy*, p. 289.

achievable. Schopenhauer similarly believes in the realization or self-knowledge of the will and affirms in Book 4 of *WWR* the possibility of a life free of subservience to the will . He cites the exemplary lives of ascetics, mystics, *sadhus* and *samanas* who live such a denial by converting from the common *samsaric* existence. This is the born-again holy life of will's denial, rare but very much real. The fourth noble truth recommends an eightfold path, a program of the removal of craving at eight different fronts of human existence:

> This, O monks, is the noble truth of the way that leads to the cessation of *dukkha:* this is the noble eight-fold path, namely, right views, right intention, right speech, right action, right livelihood, right effort, right mindfulness, right concentration … .

It is not by doing one specific thing that *nirvana* is one's due, but thinking, living, acting, speaking, intentions, meditations, all must be made moderate, calm and conducive. For the term translated as "right" happens to be *samma*, which also means moderate, well-balanced and appropriate. Although Schopenhauer's pen-portraits of the lives of the deniers of the will-to-live include similar virtues and efforts in various departments of life, he misses the element of moderation and the golden mean in Buddhism. Perhaps Schopenhauer paid only scant attention to the words of the Buddha which were spoken as a prelude to the first sermon:

> These two extremes, O monks, are not to be practised by one who has gone forth from *samsara.* What are the two? That conjoined with passions, low, common, ignoble and useless and that conjoined with self-torture, painful, ignoble and useless. Avoiding these two extremes the *Tathagata* (the Buddha or thus-arrived one) has gained the knowledge of the middle way, which gives sight and knowledge, and tends to calm, to insight, enlightenment, *nirvana.*

Thus the extremes of thoughtlessly vulgar life of *samsara* and the extreme of self-torturing asceticism are both to be avoided. The Buddha recommends a middle path both in thinking and living. In thought, metaphysical philosophizing and theistic foundations are to be given up, and the trap of nihilism (*charvaka*-type materialistic philosophy) is to be avoided. In higher living neither the life of passion, nor the life of extreme asceticism is warranted. It is obvious that Schopenhauer does not have the typically Buddhist view of asceticism, a practice which he seems to romanticize and greatly admires. Thus Schopenhauer's pessimism as well as his idealization of extreme asceticism, are not to be found in genuine Buddhism.

Nevertheless, the contribution of Schopenhauer to the introduction of Indian philosophy in the West is not to be measured by the correctness or incorrectness of his interpretations. It is his trans-cultural experiments, his new universalism, his capacity to move with remarkable ease from West to East and vice-versa, his ability to use philosophically the religious materials, that is original and praiseworthy. Helen Zimmern, one of the earliest biographers of Schopenhauer puts it very eloquently:

> It is … indispensable to appreciate clearly Schopenhauer's expression in western forms of ideas, which, originally oriental, have wandered far from their birthplace, like seeds

wafted by the winds, to germinate anew in the mind of Europe. Schopenhauer will ever stand prominent among those who have advanced and clarified the conception of the universe as unity; and even if the characteristic form in which he embodied it fails to maintain its place as the most accurate, it will nonetheless surely rank among the most impressive and sublime.[22]

Indian philosophy is all the more richer with the contribution made by Schopenhauer. He transmitted its insights in western metaphor as no one else did. At the same time, perhaps no other philosopher can combine more skillfully the seriousness of a philosophical problem with the simplicity and beauty of expression. This is how he sums up the problem and lessons of death in full sympathy with the eastern way of thinking: "You are ceasing to be something which you would have done better never to become" (*W*, II, 501).

---

22 Helen Zimmern, Schopenhauer: His Life and Philosophy (London: George Allen and Unwin, 1932), p. 14.

Chapter 5

Schopenhauer:
The Supplementary Essays

Schopenhauer intentionally maintained the cohesiveness of his system of philosophy and purposely revolved all his writings around his chief work, *The World as Will and Representation* (*WWR*), published in 1819. What was added as supplements to the four books of his original work was presented as Volume II of *WWR* in the second edition, published in 1844. The two books published earlier, *On the Will in Nature* (1836) and *The Two Problems of Ethics* (1844), were also meant to be supplements to the *magnum opus* (*W*, II, 191, 461) Thus in the preface to the "supplements to the Fourth Book" which constitutes Part 4 of Volume II of *WWR* (second edition), Schopenhauer exhorts his serious readers: "Whoever wishes to make himself acquainted with my philosophy shall read every line of me. For I am not a prolific writer, a fabricator of compendiums, an earner of fees … I have therefore written little but this little with reflection and at long intervals" (*W*, II, 461).

Schopenhauer mentions in this preface that since the ethical considerations contained in Book IV of his main work have already been supplemented by *The Two Problems of Ethics*, he has more space here to devote to the matters pertaining to the affirmation of the will-to-live, especially the reflections on "the inner significance and real nature of sexual love, a subject untouched in our fourth book itself [and] … entirely neglected by all philosophers before" (*W*, II, 462). Thus Part 4 of Volume II of *WWR* offers valuable additions to what is discussed in Book IV of the original treatise on the subject of death and contemplation, as well as new considerations on the affirmation of the will-to-live that the flesh is heir to and which manifests itself in sexual passion. This sexual passion often raises its head in the form of a deep attachment that characterizes the love between the sexes. The denial of the will-to-live and the control of sexual passion are certainly interconnected, according to Schopenhauer. It is interesting to reflect on the connection that Schopenhauer identifies between death, sexuality and salvation. He offers remarkably thoughtful insights on these deeply existential matters.

In this chapter, which is focused on the Supplementary Essays, and the next on the Later Essays of Schopenhauer, new insights on the issue of death and contemplation are to be found. These insights need to be analyzed and exposed in a comprehensive fashion and with due attention to the part played by the eastern concepts. Such interpretations are hardly available in the current secondary literature on Schopenhauer in English. We have purposely confined ourselves to the published writings of Schopenhauer. Although *Der Handschriftlicher Nachlass* (*Manuscript*

Remains) of Schopenhauer's unpublished notes, diaries, letters and writings are now available in English translation, a consideration of these materials would not have added any radically new insights on Schopenhauer's standpoints and would have lengthened our account considerably.

The quotation from Lao-Tse given at the supplements to Book IV hits the nail on the head: "all men desire solely to free themselves from death; they do not know how to free themselves from life" (*W*, II, 459). The insight that one ought to free oneself from the cravings, temptations and entanglements of life is the chief lesson of death-contemplation.

Chapter 41, entitled "On Death and its Relation to the Indestructibility of our Inner Nature," is placed at the very beginning of the supplements to Book IV which comprise the last part of Volume II of *WWR*. Schopenhauer mentions in the very first paragraph of this essay that it is quite in order that a special consideration of this subject (that is, of death) to "have its place here at the beginning of the last, most serious and most important of the books" (that is, the book that deals with the denial of the will-to-live). This remark of Schopenhauer indicates once again the central importance he assigns to death-contemplation, which must be part and parcel of any serious philosophical project dealing with human existence. This also indicates that death-contemplation penetrates the essentials of his own philosophical system.

Schopenhauer's Essay on Death

"On Death and its Relation to the Indestructibility of Our Inner Nature" is not merely a supplement to Chapter 54 of Volume I of *WWR* but an outstanding contribution to thanatology in its own right. The treatment of the issue of death given here shows Schopenhauer the philosopher and the writer at his best. Not only is he able to elucidate human being's typical concerns and attitudes toward its own mortality but also brilliantly outlines the deeper connection between the reflection on death and philosophizing as such.

The opening lines of the essay says it all: "Death is the real inspiring genius or muse of philosophy and for this reason Socrates defined philosophy as *thanatoi meletos* (rehearsal for death). Indeed without death, there would hardly have been any philosophizing" (*W*, II, 463). By calling death the real inspiration for philosophy and the philosopher, in a way, a practitioner of death, Schopenhauer seems to elucidate the classical Socratean insight concerning death and philosophy. "Indeed without death, there would hardly have been any philosophizing" can be transcribed in Schopenhauerian terms as: reflection (knowledge) in its purity is a challenge to and a triumph over the blind will-to-live to which we are subservient as a matter of course. The truth of death inspires a reflective mind to rise above the mundane, customary and stereotypical interpretations and adopt a philosophical, that is, a wholistic, ontological and extraordinary point of view. Thought of death is an eclipse of the mundane. The cycle of worldliness or *samsara* stops as if to make room for a transcendental perspective of things, when reflection is touched by what Schopenhauer calls "the terrible certainty of death."

As we have seen, for Schopenhauer this Socratean insight concerning the connection between death and philosophy is not merely a theoretical proposition. It penetrates his own philosophical work insofar as it is not only visible in its basic concept of the will-to-live and its ethical counterpart the denial of the will-to-live, but also shows itself in the basic project of his system, namely, to outline a notion of secular saturation from a frustrating meaninglessness of worldly living and worldly thinking. Schopenhauer's de-emphasis for the *samsara*-based outlook is visible not only in his work in the form of the so-called "pessimistic" standpoint so striking for many of his readers used to unnormative and cosmocentric modern western philosophy, but also visible in the way Schopenhauer led his own life. Indeed to misunderstand Schopenhauer's standpoint on *samsara* is to misunderstand the colourful but determined life of the man.

In this essay, Schopenhauer maintains that philosophy not only becomes truly itself, or genuine in its encounter with death, but it also provides an antidote to the terrible certainty, the fearsome loss that death represents to a mind not yet consoled by the metaphysical points of view. Schopenhauer devotes the bulk of this essay to bringing home the truth that the will-to-live that is our inner nature is indestructible. He explains why it is so, by exposing the relationship between the individual and the species. Thus the essay deals with the consolation that the Schopenhauerian philosophy offers in the face of death. However, this antidote is not merely offered as a therapy but clothed in a strong philosophical argument. At the same time, the connection between contemplation and death continues to unfold throughout the essay. The role of philosophy as a consolation against death is referred to in the following inimitable words by Schopenhauer:

> The animal lives without any real knowledge of death … with man the terrifying certainty of death necessarily appeared along with the faculty of reason. But … the same reflection that introduced the knowledge of death also assists us in obtaining "metaphysical" points of view … All religions and philosophical systems are directed principally to this end and are thus primarily the antidote to the certainty of death which reflecting reason produces from its own resources. The degree in which they attain this end is, however, very different, and one religion or philosophy will certainly enable man, far more than others will, to look death calmly in the face. [*W*, II, 463]

Schopenhauer shows a distinct preference for Vedanta and Buddhism in this regard, for Vedanta contains the insight that our inner core is *brahman* the imperishable, and Buddhism offers the ultimate salvation of *nirvana*. However, Schopenhauer has little regard for religious traditions that teach that man "came but recently from nothing, that consequently he has been nothing throughout an eternity … although he is through and through the work of another, he shall nevertheless be responsible to all eternity for his commissions and omissions" (*W*, II, 464). The religions that teach this human origin out of nothing include Judaism, Old Testament Christianity and Islam, whereas Schopenhauer keeps New Testament Christianity in a class apart, for it seems to him to be not only close to Hinduism but also inspired by it with respect to its concept of the original sin, its condemnation of worldliness and its concept of moral responsibility, and so on.

Concerning the issue of the possibility of immortality, Schopenhauer remarks, "In Europe, the opinion of men ... vacillates afresh between the conception of death as absolute annihilation and the assumption that we are, so to speak with skin and hair, immortal. Both are equally false" (*W*, II, 464). It is precisely these two assumptions that Schopenhauer wishes to correct in this essay. His larger view of death and immortality is rooted in what he calls the will-to-live, or the ontological reality that pervades everything that lives. This will-to-live is irrational, blind and a force to be reckoned with, characterized by an urge to live, sustain itself and survive. Survive it does in the species if not in and as the individual. It is the task of Schopenhauer's essay to argue that we can claim an immortality of sorts due to the fact that our inner core, namely the will-to-live, clearly seems to realize its urge to live and continue. In his study of the perpetuation of the species, Schopenhauer takes a truly larger view of life and warns that "We shall have false notions about the indestructibility of our true nature through death, so long as we do not make up our minds to study it first of all in the animals, and claim for ourselves alone a class apart from them under the boastful name of immortality" (*W*, II, 482).

A proper study of will-to-live requires that we pay attention to our own animality as well as that of the animals. Once again, Schopenhauer embraces the Vedic and Buddhist notions of human kinship with the animal kingdom, both in terms of their myth of reincarnation as well as the theory of karma. However, for the most part he attempts to outline the empirical evidence for the fact that will-to-live perpetuates itself in the species and that nature has little regard for the individual living being, be it human or animal.

Schopenhauer begins his analysis of death by pointing toward the fear of death that exists in all living things (*W*, II, 464). The fact that human beings fear death of their own person more than anything else, regard death of the other as a great misfortune, or as the greatest punishment to be inflicted on the enemy all point to the belief that death is annihilation:

> Such fear of death, however, is a priori the reverse side of will-to-live, which indeed we all are ... Why does the animal flee, tremble and try to conceal itself? Because it is simply the will-to-live, but as such it is forfeit to death and would like to gain time. By nature man is just the same. The greatest of evils, the worst thing that can threaten anywhere, is death; the greatest anxiety is the anxiety of death. Nothing excites us so irresistibly to the most lively interest as does the danger to the lives of others; nothing is more dreadful than an execution. Now the boundless attachment to life that appears here cannot have sprung from knowledge and reflection. To these, on the contrary it appears foolish, for the objective value of life is very uncertain, and it remains at least doubtful whether existence is to be preferred to non-existence; in fact, if experience and reflection have their say, non-existence must certainly win. [*W*, II, 465]

The fear of death is rooted in will-to-live, and not in any rational principle, according to Schopenhauer. To knowledge which is an "adventitious principle," fear of death appears foolish:

> Knowledge ... far from being the origin of that attachment to life, even opposes it, since it discloses life's worthlessness, in this way combats the fear of death, when it is victorious, and man accordingly faces death courageously and calmly, this is honoured as great and noble. Therefore, we then extol the triumph of knowledge over the blind will-to-live ... In the same way we despise him in whom knowledge is defeated in that conflict, who therefore clings unconditionally to life, struggle to the utmost against approaching death, and receives it with despair. [*W*, II, 466]

Schopenhauer's reference to a conflict between the blind will-to-live and knowledge is itself rooted in his pessimistic interpretation of the fundamental doctrine of Vedanta and Buddhism that *samsara* (the world life-cycle) ought not to be perpetuated and salvation (*moksha* or *nirvana*) is characterized by a final cessation of having to exist. Hence true and highest knowledge (which Vedanta calls *jnana*) is a liberation from mundane existence. Schopenhauer's statements, such as "the objective value of life is very uncertain," "it is doubtful whether existence is to be preferred to non-existence," "knowledge discloses life's worthlessness," are not merely by-products of his pessimism but also rooted in his deeper appreciation of the fundamental presuppositions of the eastern world-view which expresses a disdain of *samsara* religiously, mythologically and philosophically. This view is so succinctly put into words by Schopenhauer: "at bottom we are something that ought not to be. Therefore, we cease to be" (*W*, II, 507).

Whereas Schopenhauer extols the truth-value of basic Vedanta and Buddhist doctrines, especially those that Vedanta and Buddhism share in common and the ones that are remarkably distinct from the Judeo-Christian and Islamic pre-suppositions, he interprets these in his own somewhat pessimistic way. The belief that human being ought to overcome its matter-of-course attachment with and value of *samsara* does not mean that life is worthless, according to Vedanta. Human life is at the same time an opportunity to let knowledge triumph over *maya*, or will-to-live, and thus valuable, and it is deemed priceless among all other existences for that reason. Schopenhauer expresses these ideas in his own characteristic profound manner: "death is a serious matter could already be inferred from the fact that, as everyone knows life is no joke. Indeed we must not deserve anything better than these two" (*W*, II, 465). Life as well as death are serious challenges to us, that no one can deny. But what does Schopenhauer mean when he remarks "indeed we must not deserve anything better" than such a life and such a death? This has echoes of the Vedic and Buddhist belief that having to be born and having to die is not a good thing, the wise must seek liberation from the cycle of *samsara* by accumulating merit of *karma*, or acts that show detachment from *samsara* and egolessness. Of course, what is mythologically expressed in terms of reincarnation or continuing cycle of births and deaths, has deep existential moral implications. As exposed in the *Katha Upanishad*, the higher life (*samprye*) of one who contemplates the meaning of death does not necessarily mean the next life. The life of thoughtless subservience to *maya* and life of lived-knowledge are both possible in this very life. However, Schopenhauer seems to accept the Vedic and Buddhist myth of reincarnation quite literally because he finds it both quite logical in its own right and consistent with his own reading of the activity of will-to-will to perpetuate itself, which he finds evident all over in nature. At the same time he points out that reincarnation is a belief held by non-western people all over the world:

> We find the doctrine of metempsychosis, springing from the very earliest and noblest ages of the human race, always world-wide, as the belief of the great majority of mankind, in fact really as the doctrine of all religions, with the exception of Judaism and the two religions that have arisen from it … We find this doctrine in its subtlest form, coming nearest to the truth, in Buddhism. [*W*, II, 504]

Schopenhauer has special affinity with the Buddhist notion of rebirth, which is based on the assumption that there is no soul to transmigrate and whereas the new birth is a karmic consequence of the old, it is not a continuation of the old personality. That he finds the Vedic world-view also quite convincing is visible in the following profound words: "we might say to the dying individual: you are ceasing to be something which you would have done better never to become" (*W*, II, 501).

Schopenhauer does not accept the Judeo-Christian concept of human being's creation out of nothing and finds the issue of non-existence after death essentially linked with that of the non-existence before birth. He finds it hard to accept the common notion of death as absolute annihilation and the birth as absolute beginning:

> An entire infinity ran its course when we did not yet exist but this in no way disturbs us. On the other hand, we find it hard, even unendurable, that after the momentary intermezzo of an ephemeral existence, a second infinity should follow in which we shall exist "no longer". How could this thirst for existence possibly have arisen through our having tasted it and found it very delightful … Notwithstanding all this, the question of our state after death has certainly been discussed verbally and in books ten thousand times more often than our state before birth. [*W*, II, 467]

Instead of taking the issue of the aftermath of death from the standpoint of an individual's short life-span, Schopenhauer considers the big picture as he rejects the notion of creation of anybody and anything out of nothing, taking all existence and non-existence as part of a causal sequence in which will-to-live affirms itself, perpetuates itself by preserving the species and by being indifferent to individual existences. Schopenhauer's acceptance of the classical Hindu and Buddhist notion of *samsara* as a life-death world cycle, the causality of *karma* theory and the Buddhist notion of dependent origination is quite apparent here. He finds these doctrines quite consistent with his own secular account of the inner workings of the will-to-live. He admires the logical consistency of Vedanta and Buddhism in the following words:

> All proofs of continued existence after death may also be applied just as well *in partem ante*, where they then demonstrate existence before life, in assuming which the Hindus

and Buddhists therefore show themselves to be very consistent … But quite apart even from these considerations of time, it is in and by itself absurd to regard non-existence as an evil. [*W*, II, 467]

It may be noted that Schopenhauer does not merely invoke the support of the eastern philosophies for his philosophical insights but relies primarily on the empirical evidence he cites to back up his claims concerning inner patterns of the will-to-live. How far the eastern concepts have shaped and enriched the details provided in his later supplementary writings is an open question.

Schopenhauer points out that there is evidence for the conclusion that non-existence is no evil: "Just as sleep is the brother of death, fainting fit its twin brother" (*W*, II, 468). In the *Brahadaranyaka Upanishad* (4, 3, 7), an extended analysis of sleep, dreamless sleep and death is given of which Schopenhauer must have been aware since, for many years, he kept a copy of Anquetil Duperon's *Oupnekhat* by his bedside. Sleep is described in this *Upanishad*, as especially revelatory of the nature of *samsara* and of the release from it: "Verily there are two conditions of this person: the condition of being in this world and the condition of being in the other world. There is an intermediate third condition, namely, that of being in sleep. By standing in this intermediate condition one sees both these conditions" (4, 3, 9).

The experience of losing consciousness reveals even more than that of sleep that the sensation brought about by these is anything but unpleasant:

> From this it may be concluded that the entire cessation of life-process must be a wonderful relief for its driving force. Perhaps this is partly responsible for the expression of sweet contentment on the faces of most of the dead. In general, the moment of dying may be similar to that of waking from a heavy nightmare. [*W*, II, 469]

Of course there is a fine line between the de-emphasis of *samsara*, to which Vedanta and Buddhism are committed, and downright condemnation and rejection of *samsara*, to which Schopenhauer's pessimistic outlook on human life seems very often to sink. The last statement of the above quote seems to echo Socrates' famous last words "Crito, we ought to offer a cock to Asclepius. See to it, and don't forget"[1] as reported in the *Phaedo*.

Schopenhauer devotes the bulk of the rest of this essay to providing the empirical evidence for his assertion that the cessation of individual lives must not be regarded either as "the annihilation of the living principle" or as "the entire destruction of man":

> We know, of course, of no higher gamble than that for life and death. We watch with utmost attention, interest and fear every decision concerning them; for in our view all in all is at stake. On the other hand Nature, which never lies, but is always frank and sincere, speaks quite differently on this theme, as Krishna does in the *Bhagavadgita*. Her statement is that the life or death of the individual is of absolutely no consequence. She expresses this

---

1 Plato, *Phaedo*, 118a.

by abandoning the life of every animal, even of man to the most insignificant accidents without coming to the rescue. [*W*, II, 473]

Schopenhauer refers to the important lesson that the thoughtful person must draw from this: "The life and death of the individual is a matter of indifference to [nature]. Consequently they should be, in a certain sense, a matter of indifference to us, for in fact, we ourselves are nature" (*W*, II, 474). At the same time, we witness the fate of living things all around us. Wherever there is life, death is near at hand. Whereas individuals perish the species seem to remain intact:

> Everything lingers only for a moment, and hurries on to death. The plant and insect die at the end of the summer, the animal and man after a few years; death reaps unweariedly. But despite all this, in fact as if this were not the case at all, everything is always there and in its place, just as everything was imperishable … [E]ach and everything that "wills" to exist actually does exist continuously and without end. Accordingly, at any given point of time all species of animals, from gnat to the elephant, exist together complete … It is the species that always lives and the individuals cheerfully exist in the consciousness of the imperishability of the species and their identity with it. Death is for the species what sleep is for the individual, or winking for the eye. [*W*, II, 479]

Schopenhauer seems to ignore the fact that species too have a life of their own and, at times, are known to have become extinct. But one species can be viewed as giving rise to another at the time of its own extinction. The remark "the individuals cheerfully exist in the consciousness of the imperishability of species and their identity with it" echoes Schopenhauer's explanation in *WWR*, Volume I (p. 282) of the human self-assurance concerning death and the habitual dismissal of one's own death as a theoretical fact. This calmness and indifference toward one's own death, which Heidegger considers as the inauthentic attitude toward death, was attributed by Schopenhauer to a deeper instinctual and animal like conviction in man's Being or a gut feeling that something in us is imperishable and always endowed with a living present.

Death is a matter having to do with the human–world relationship. How one takes the human–world connection to be has implications for one's understanding of death. Schopenhauer warns that human being and its world should not be taken in the sense of a simplistic subject–object relation. He remarks that

> … fundamentally we are far at one with the world than we usually think, its inner nature is our will, and its phenomenal appearance our representation. The difference between the continuance of the eternal world after his death and his own continuance after death would vanish for anyone who could bring this unity or identity of being to distinct consciousness. [*W*, II, 487]

Although it will be simplistic to equate Schopenhauer's concept of the will-to-live with *maya* and/or *brahman*, the influence of Vedanta philosophy is unmistakable in his understanding of the human–world relation. We are reminded for instance that "the world is no less in us than we are in it, and the source of all reality lies with us"

(*W*, II, 487). At the same time Schopenhauer offers a potent argument: "This center of all existence, this kernel of all reality, is to be abolished, and yet the world is to be allowed to go on existing; it is an idea that may of course, be conceived in the abstract, but not realized" (*W*, II, 487). The Vedantic insight that brahman is the soul (*atman*) of all existents, and that the inner and the outer reality is one, is echoed in Schopenhauer's statement that "world is no less in us than we are in it."

What is crucial in our understanding of death is whether or not we take ourselves to be necessary beings, whether or not we believe that whatever exists, necessarily exists. This issue is also closely related to the question concerning the creation out of nothing as well as concerning continued causal origination, which are but a matter of religious belief. Schopenhauer repeatedly shows his preference for the Vedantic and Buddhist notions of endless *samsara* originating on the basis of the theory of *karma*, as well as the Buddhist notion of dependent origination over the Judeo-Christian doctrine of one's creation out of nothing at the hands of a creator God:

> The assumption that man is created out of nothing necessarily leads to the assumption that death is his absolute end. In this respect, therefore, the Old Testament is quite consistent; for no doctrine of immortality is appropriate to a creation out of nothing. New Testament Christianity has such a doctrine because it is Indian in spirit, and therefore more than probably, Indian in origin, although only indirectly, through Egypt … Brahmanism and Buddhism, on the other hand, quite consistently with continued existence after death, have an existence before birth, and the purpose of this life to atone for the guilt of that previous existence. Therefore, if considerations of this kind are certainly calculated to awaken the conviction that there is something in us that death cannot destroy, this nevertheless happens only by our being raised to a point of view from which birth is not the beginning of our existence. [*W*, II, 488, 490]

"There is something in us that death cannot destroy": in Schopenhauerian terms, this means that the will-to-live is indestructible and perpetuates itself in the life of the species. For the will cares less for the individual, even though it is the reason we love life to the utmost, wish to preserve ourselves at all costs, love ourselves and express our attachment for the world and things worldly. This is why the denial of the will-to-live is the essence of true wisdom and true religion and reflects itself in the lives of genuine philosophers, saints and spiritual masters from both eastern and western traditions, as outlined by Schopenhauer in the Book IV of Volume I of *WWR*. The immortality that is desired and realized by the wise is never the immortality of their individuality: "To desire immortality for the individual is to perpetuate an error for ever; for at bottom every individuality is really only a special error, a false step, something that it would be better should not be, in fact something from which it is the real purpose of life to bring us back" (*W*, II, 492).

This is a kind of assertion that puzzles those readers of Schopenhauer who are unfamiliar with eastern thought. In the secondary literature, such claims of

Schopenhauer have been called "absurd" or "perverse" by some commentators.[2] In fact, there is nothing absurd or perverse about Schopenhauer's appreciation of the Vedantic and Buddhist assumption that having to be reborn in *samsara* is no event for celebration. The bliss of *nirvana* must be a contrast to the unsatisfactoriness and vulgarity of a *samsaric* existence. Otherwise, this would mean, in Schopenhauerian terms, the dismissal of the fact that the will-to-live lives on and the acceptance of the notion that death is one's absolute annihilation. The real purpose of human life is to overcome the individuality-based, narrow-minded thinking that affirms *samsara*. According to Schopenhauer, death is largely misunderstood and mistakenly described as fearsome, for

> The terrors of death rest for the most part on the false illusion that then the I or ego vanishes, and the world remains. But rather is the opposite true, namely that the world vanishes; on the other hand, the innermost kernel of the ego endures, the bearer and the producer of the subject in whose representation alone the world has its existence ... Yet it is he who despairs in the individual who suffers the dread of death, since he is exposed to the illusion, produced by the *principium individuationis*, that his existence is limited to the being that is now dying. This illusion is part of the heavy dream into which he, as will-to-live has fallen. However, we might say to the dying individual: "you are ceasing to be something which you would have done better never to become". [*W*, II, 500, 501]

Schopenhauer is referring to the enigmatic reality of the world, which is both the subjective and the objective for us. Death is usually taken as a removal or departure of oneself from the world that will go on existing. But if the subjective status of the world is recognized and it is taken as a network of meanings created by and used by an individual mind, then that world, the only world that the individual has known, must cease with that individual's death. And yet "the innermost kernel of the ego" what Schopenhauer calls will-to-live and Vedanta calls *atman*, "the bearer and producer of the subject" remains and endures as the soul of all existents. The spell of the Vedanta philosophy along with that of its concepts of *atman* and *maya* is unmistakable in Schopenhauer's understanding of the *principium individuationis*, in his references to *maya* as illusion and heavy dream, and in his account of death as ceasing to be something which one would have done better never to become. This means in existential terms that one would have done better to have looked beyond the veil of *maya* and risen above the narrower life of self-love and pursuit of worldliness. In mythological terms, the same thing is described as one ought to have done better to avoid the cycle of rebirth and having to remain caught up in *samsara*.

The world cannot be described as merely the external world composed of all existent objects, as Descartes took it to mean. Nor can it be described as merely

---

2   For example, M. Fox in "Schopenhauer on Death, Suicide and Self-Renunciation" in M. Fox (ed.), *Schopenhauer: His Philosophical Achievement* (New York: Barnes and Noble, 1980).

subjective, existing solely in the subject's head. Schopenhauer's statement on the first page of *WWR*, namely "this world is my representation," leans on the subjective while correcting the common notion of the world as merely the sum-total of objects. However, Schopenhauer serves as a predecessor to Heidegger in exposing the problem of the world-concept (*Weltbegriffe*) in a comprehensive way and in correcting the commonplace notion of the world as a mere container of entities. Unlike Heidegger, who has an exclusively existential notion of the world, Schopenhauer while intertwining his notion with that of *samsara* subscribes to the metaphysical, religious and mythological aspects of the world and mortals who enter and exist it. Schopenhauer sums up the essence of his own thought in the following statement on the connection between the world and death: "From the metaphysical standpoint the sentences 'I perish but the world endures' and 'the world perishes and I endure' are not really different at bottom" (*W*, II, 507).

The chief lesson of death, Schopenhauer sums up as "death is the great opportunity no longer to be I; to him, of course who embraces it." The existential teaching of death exhorts us to rise above self-love and love of the world and deny what people call "the good life," what Vedanta calls the entanglements of *maya* and *moha*.

Schopenhauer profoundly describes death as a reprimand and punishment well deserved for most of us who approach life thoughtlessly; who do not look the will-to-live in the eye: "Death is the great reprimand that the will-to-live and more particularly the egoism essential thereto, receive through the course of nature; and it can be conceived as a punishment for our existence ... At bottom, we are something that ought not to be, therefore we cease to be" (*W*, II, 507).

The statement "at bottom we are something that ought not to be" can be misunderstood as a downright pessimism. It must be analyzed in the light of the dismissal of *samsara* that, according to Vedanta and Buddhism, every thoughtful human must cultivate, a notion which is both admired and incorporated into his own system by Schopenhauer. Death is part of the process of growing out of *samsara*, or remaining forever caught up in it and receiving punishment time and again for missing out on *nirvana*. Schopenhauer recalls the great statement that Socrates made, through his life and death, and subsumes it with what the *Upanishadic* seers sought from knowledge (*jnana*), to be led from death to deathlessness, what Buddhism calls the march from *samsara* to *nirvana*:

> As a rule, the death of every good person is peaceful and gentle, but to die willingly, to die gladly, to die cheerfully, is the prerogative of the resigned, him who gives up and denies the will-to-live. For he alone wishes to die actually and not merely apparently and consequently needs and desires no continuance of his person. He willingly gives up the existence that we know; what comes to him instead of it is in our eyes "nothing", because our existence in reference to that one is "nothing". The Buddhist faith calls that existence *nirvana*. [*W*, II, 508]

The central importance of death-contemplation in the conception and living of philosophy is visible in many ways in Schopenhauer's work. The concept of will-to-live and its denial are the pivotal notions in Schopenhauer's system and their connection with death and death-contemplation is obvious. The reality of death is a challenge to the matter-of-course pursuit of the will-to-live. Philosophy and the philosophical life are shown as inspired responses to the terrible certainty of death by Schopenhauer. The denial of the will-to-live is a welcome voluntary adoption, acceptance and practice of death in one's life. It is the life of a genuine philosopher, as Socrates conceived it. Among other things it prepares one not only for philosophy but also for one's actual death, for which the philosophical life is a rehearsal. According to Schopenhauer, death-contemplation and the contemplative life also prepare one to have a glimpse of salvation, as one may become a candidate for *nirvana*.

In Book 4 of Volume II of *WWR*, Schopenhauer continues to elaborate on the problems and the chief concepts identified in the essay on death. Several essays that follow contain the considerations of the problems directly related to the meaning of death. "The Life of the Species," "The Metaphysics of Sexual Love," "On the Affirmation of the Will-to-Live," "On the Vanity and Suffering of Life," "On the Doctrine of the Denial of the Will-to-Live" and "The Road to Salvation" all contain not only frequent references to death but also supplementary analyses of the allied problems first discussed in Book IV of the original Volume I of *WWR*.

The Life of the Species

In the essay on death, an argument was presented concerning the imperishability of the inner nature of the human being, resting on the fact that nature seems to care less for the individual but undeniably preserves the species. Schopenhauer attributes human confidence against the threat of death, and the seeming forgetfulness of death in one's daily living, to the inner knowledge that all humans are endowed with, namely, that death poses no threat to their will-to-live which is bound to survive in the continuation of the species. In the essay entitled "The Life of the Species," further comments are made on the all-important issue of the indestructibility of the species, as well as on the remarkable care taken by nature, including the human nature to ensure the continuation of the species. The following exposition of human nature is given in this very essay which explains why sexual love as well as the love of progeny is all important to human beings:

> Although the will attains self-consciousness only in the individual, yet the deep-seated consciousness that it is really the species in which its true being objectifies itself appears in the fact that the affairs of the species as such, i.e. the relation of the sexes, the generation and nourishment of the offspring are to the individual of comparably greater important and consequence than anything else. [*W*, II, 510]

It may seem to us that our individual and selfish concerns are most important to us. In fact, the affairs of the species such as the generation and upbringing of the offspring as well as sexual selection and pursuits are far more important to human beings.[3] In this respect, humans behave as instinctively as animals, albeit among humans, both sexual matters and parental love are "guided and directed by the faculty of reason [or] reflection" (*W*, II, 514), which enhances their sophistication but does not diminish their strength. Schopenhauer reiterates his insight that:

> Sexual impulse is the kernel of the will-to-live and consequently the concentration of all willing. In the text [*WWR*] therefore I have called the genitals the focus of the will. Indeed it may be said that man is concrete sexual impulse, for his origin is an act of copulation … It is true that the will-to-live manifests itself primarily as an effort to maintain the individual; yet this is only a stage towards the effort to maintain the species. [*W*, II, 514]

It is not hard to see here why Schopenhauer's philosophy was influential in the development of Freud's theories concerning human sexuality. Schopenhauer illustrates as well as explains the vehemence of the sexual impulse by tracing its origins in the all-important issue of the continuation of the species. There is then a connection between sexuality and immortality, or at least between it and a craving and a drive toward overcoming the terrible certainty of death. Schopenhauer brilliantly and graphically describes the omnipresence of this core of all willing:

> This is the important role played by the sex-relation in the world of mankind, where it is really the invisible central point of all action and conduct, and peeps up everywhere, in spite of all the veils thrown over it. It is the cause of war and the aim and object of peace, the basis of the serious and the aim of the joke, the inexhaustible source of wit, the key to all hints and allusions, and the meaning of all secret signs and suggestions, all unexpressed proposals, and all stolen glances; it is the daily thought and desire of the young and often of the old as well, the hourly thought of the unchaste, and the constantly recurring reverie of the chaste against their will, the ever ready material for a joke, only because the profoundest seriousness lies at its root. [*W*, II, 513]

Schopenhauer expands on this connection between sexuality and the inner design of the will-to-live to perpetuate the species in his essay "The Metaphysics of Sexual Love," which follows his highly speculative piece on "The Hereditary Nature of Qualities," which in turn is based on his belief that one inherits intellect from one's mother and will from one's father. To posit and root human qualities and pre-dispositions in heredity is in accord with Schopenhauer's tendency to de-emphasize the individual and the individual's current existence and its experiences, and to assert the role of generation and the species. It is also in tune with the Buddhist belief that pre-dispositions (*svabhava*) are inherited on the basis of the *karma* of past lives rather than being an exclusive by-product of one's current life and its experiences. In any case, Schopenhauer's attribution of will to the father and intellect to the mother seems to be not only an oversimplification but also an outdated and scientifically unproven assertion.

---

3   These are misunderstood as individual concerns, whereas they are truly the matters pertaining to the species.

The Metaphysics of Sexual Love

Schopenhauer begins this essay by pointing out that "this chapter is the last of the four, and their varied and mutual references to one another, by virtue of which they form to a certain extent a subordinate whole, will be recognized by the attentive reader (*W*, II, 531). This means that death, life of the species, hereditary nature of qualities and sexual love, the very phenomena that are the subject-matter of these four chapters, have much to do with each other intimately. It will be interesting to discover not only the connection between sexual love and the life of the species but also between sexual love and death as elucidated by Schopenhauer in this essay.

Sexual love and its nature is a constant theme of the works of poets and dramatists and accepted by their readership with deep interest. It is also well known that this "lively yet still controllable inclination can, in certain circumstances grow to be a passion exceeding every other in intensity"(*W*, II, 532). Schopenhauer expresses the regret that "a matter that generally plays so important a part in the life of man has hitherto been almost entirely disregarded by philosophers." Whatever little is treated in the odd discourses on the subject by the likes of Plato, Kant and Spinoza is inadequate, naïve and peripheral. Thus Schopenhauer believes that he is the first thinker to treat this important human activity seriously, comprehensively and truly philosophically. This is perhaps another example of traditional philosophy for the most part being preoccupied with abstract and non-existential themes. Thus Schopenhauer rightly claims that he has no predecessors in this philosophical treatment of sexual love.

The first assertion that Schopenhauer makes is that "all amorousness is rooted in the sexual impulse alone, is in fact absolutely only a more closely determined, specialized and indeed in the strictest sense individualized sexual impulse, however ethereally it may deport itself' (*W*, II, 533). This means that love between two individuals of the opposite sex is always the sexual love, however, non-sexual it may be understood and presented by the lovers to themselves or others. It is an intense and fixed sexual desire for a specific beloved individual. It is pursued with a seriousness so profound that it astonishes the persons concerned. Unbeknownst to the individuals fallen into this passion, the realization of the deepest aims of the species gets underway in the pursuits of love:

> The ultimate aim of all love-affairs, whether played in sock or in buskin, is actually more important than all other aims in man's life; and therefore it is quite worthy of the profound seriousness with which everyone pursues it. What is decided by it is nothing less than the composition of the next generation. [*W*, I, 534]

Thus the couple in love is entirely subjected to the aim of the will-to-live to perpetuate itself. What Schopenhauer asserts is that the real reason a love affair is happening is that a child is to be born. Two individuals of the opposite sex are drawn together and find themselves deeply attached, presumably due to their liking for each other. But in fact, nature has brought them together because they could be the perfect parents of a child, whose birth would propagate the species and contribute to the ongoing objectification of the will-to-live: "The moment when the parents begin to love each other … is actually to be regarded as the very first formation of a new individual" (*W*, II, 536). Schopenhauer maintains that nature "implants in the individual a certain delusion, and by virtue of this that which in truth is merely a good thing for the species seems to him to be a good thing for himself" (*W*, I, 538). Beauty and sensual pleasure are mere instruments by which the eternal music of the renewal of the will-to-live is played. The beauty of the female form, so enticing for the male, the age, the health, the skeleton, the face are all factors in the union of the lovers. Reproduction is the single most important reason in all sexual attraction: "A full female bosom exerts an exceptional charm on the male, because, being directly connected with the woman's functions of propagation, it promises a newborn child abundant nourishment" (*W*, II, 543).

Schopenhauer gives a graphic account of his exposition of love by locating love in terms of sexuality and sexuality in terms of reproduction. He explains the seeming compatibility and incompatibility of couples in his central notion of the Being of all being, the will-to-live:

> While the lovers speak pathetically of the harmony of their souls, the core of the matter is often the agreement … with regard to the being that is to be produced and to its perfection. Moreover such agreement is obviously of much more importance than is the harmony of their souls; not long after the wedding this harmony often resolves itself in a howling discord. [*W*, II, 546]

Schopenhauer has very perceptively identified sexuality as a fundamental impulse to life. It is part and parcel of what he calls the affirmation of the will-to-live. It goes hand in hand with worldly attachments that affirmation of life and the so-called living to the fullest bestows on all human beings. Sexuality is so closely tied to the affirmation of life both here and in the interest of the hereafter, that it is part and parcel of the normalcy of the worldly existence. This is why, according to Schopenhauer, sexual abstinence, complete chastity must be the first feature of the denial of the will-to-live. In such denial, one refuses to be a puppet of the will's hidden purposes to perpetuate itself, and the ultimate undesirability of the continuation of *samsara* and one's subjection to it.

Toward the end of the essay, Schopenhauer points out the connection between this analysis of sexual love and his "metaphysics in general":

> The whole metaphysics of love here discussed is closely connected with my metaphysics in general … We have seen that, in the satisfaction of the sexual impulse, the careful selection … rests on the extremely serious interest taken by man in the personal constitution of the next generation. Now this … confirms two truths set forth in preceding chapters; (1) the indestructibility of man's true being-in-itself, which continues to live in the coming generation. For that interest … could not be present so indelibly, and exercise so great a power over man if he were absolutely perishable … (2) That his true being-in-itself lies rather in the species than in the individual. For that interest in the special constitution of the species … forms the root of all love affairs. [*W*, II, 559]

The connection between sexual love and mortality is beautifully expressed by Schopenhauer: "Why, then, does the man in love hang with complete abandon on the eyes of his chosen one, and is ready to make every sacrifice for her? Because it is his 'immortal part' that longs for her; it is always the mortal part alone that longs for everything else" (*W*, II, 559). It may be mentioned that in the cultures that hold a firm belief in reincarnation, it is very common on the part of the lovers to view their love as ranging over several life-times. They often believe that their affair truly began in a previous life-time and their true love will surpass mortality and shall continue in their future incarnations.

The matter-of-course continuation of *samsara*, with its inevitable sufferings and turmoils, and ranging over many life-spans and the rare possibility of salvation (*nirvana*), is expressed as follows by Schopenhauer in his own terminology:

> Now this is the will-to-live, and hence precisely that which has so pressing and urgent a desire for life and continuance. Accordingly, this remains immune from, and unaffected by, death. But there is also the fact that it cannot attain to a better state or condition than its present one; consequently, with life, the constant suffering and dying of individuals are certain to it. To free it from this is reserved for the 'denial' of the will-to-live; through this denial the individual will tear itself away from the stem of the species ... We lack concepts for what the will now is ... we can only describe it as that which is free to be or not to be the will-to-live. For the latter case, Buddhism describes it by the word *nirvana*. [*W*, II, 560]

Affirmation of the Will

In Chapter 45 of Volume II, Schopenhauer continues to link sexuality with the will-to-live, and takes stock of the affirmation of the will that accompanies any human life that lacks the courage for the denial:

> Since ... the will wills life absolutely and for all time, it exhibits itself at the same time as sexual impulse, which has an endless series of generations in view ...
>
> Tied up with the satisfaction of that strongest of all impulses and desires is the origin of a new existence, and hence carrying out of life afresh ... in 'another' individual ...
>
> Yet if the two, who are different in the phenomenon, were such absolutely and in themselves, where then would eternal justice be found? [*W*, II, 568]

The will does not will life merely in the here-and-now but "absolutely and for all time." Sexual impulse in the human being is a manifestation of the instinctual clinging to life which cannot be confined to one lifetime, for it seeks to conquer death by causing "origin of a new existence," even though this new existence is subject to all the suffering crowned by the death of a human life. Schopenhauer seems to be fully convinced of the Buddhist theory of rebirth (*palingenesis*) and *karma* when he affirms that any human birth must be a dependent origination, part of a causal chain, a series, or else there will be no eternal justice, that is, one's actions good or bad, thoughtful or thoughtless, will have no reward or punishment beyond one lifetime. It is not that the progeny must atone for the sins of the parents in specific cases, but on the whole the new arrivals in *samsara* come laden with some guilt and some debt; this is evidenced by the fact that the suffering and ease are not disposed by destiny in proportion to one's actions and intentions in one's current life. Bad things happen to good people, and often the evil seem to commit evil with impunity. How could misfortunes, cares and misery be one's lot on the basis of one's actions in one lifetime? It seems to Schopenhauer that coming into *samsara* itself must be a punishment and a debt to be repaid. He clearly subscribes to the notion of the affirmation of the will-to-live (*samsara*) as *maya* (illusion) and the myth of reincarnation, especially its Buddhist version (*palingenesis*):

> The life of man with its endless care, want and suffering is to be regarded as the explanation or paraphrase of the act of procreation, of the decided affirmation of the will-to-live. Further, it is also due to this that he owes to nature the debt of death, and thinks of this debt with uneasiness. Is not this evidence of the fact that our existence involves guilt? But we certainly always exist on periodic payment of the toll, birth and death, and we enjoy successively all the sorrows and joys of life, so that none can escape us. This is just the fruit of the affirmation of the will-to-live. Thus the fear of death, which holds us firmly to life in spite of all its miseries, is really illusory; but just as illusory is the impulse that has enticed us into it. [*W*, II, 569]

Thus life is described by Schopenhauer as a paraphrase of the will's affirmation; as soon as this affirmation takes place, the debt of a certain death is incurred. Man is always restless, uneasy, nervous and fearful regarding the repayment of this debt. This is the sign of the guilt that comes with existence, a guilt that arises due to a wrong choice that has been made, that is, the choice of affirming (the worldly) life rather than denying the blind will toward life.

Schopenhauer points toward the shame and guilt associated with the sexual act as well as the secretive approach toward it. These are the universal attitudes toward sex and sexuality:

> Now if optimism were right, if our existence were ... gift of the highest goodness ... praiseworthy, commendable, and delightful, then certainly the act that perpetuates it would necessarily bear quite a different complexion.
>
> If on the other hand, this existence is a kind of false step or wrong path, if it is the work of an originally blind will ... then the act perpetuating that existence must appear precisely as in fact it does. [*W*, II, 570]

The Hindu and Buddhist myths of reincarnation as well as the theory of *karma*, the theory of dependent origination along with concepts of *maya* and *trishna* (craving), with which Schopenhauer is very well conversant by the time of the writing of Volume II (1944) of the *WWR*, enable him to revalidate and supplement his system as presented in Volume I (1919). He is able to add to what he maintained in the first outline of his metaphysical system, on the basis of his vast reading of the primary and secondary texts of Indian philosophy that were becoming available in Europe in his times. It will not be an exaggeration to say that he provides a secular, rational, and philosophical explanation for the myth of reincarnation widely and literally believed by the Hindu and Buddhist masses. For example, he remarks:

> On the long path that the will, originally without knowledge, had to traverse before it rose to intellect, especially to human, rational intellect, it became such a stranger to itself; and so it no longer knows its origin ... and from the standpoint of pure, hence innocent, knowledge is horrified there at. [*W*, II, 571]

This seems to be a paraphrase of the Hindu belief in reincarnation which presents the human birth at the summit of the successive series of animal existences, the human birth being distinguished due to the very possibility it offers for leading the life of restraint and good actions (*dharma*), leading up to the possibility of salvation (*moksha*). Although Schopenhauer does mention the possibility of denial of the will and of salvation, but it is not a good enough reason to regard human existence as an optimistic event. This is where he stops listening to the true spirit of Hinduism and Buddhism, for which human existence is noble, joyful and blessed precisely because it offers a real opportunity for *dharma* and *moksha*. Schopenhauer's pessimistic interpretation celebrates the possibility of the denial and salvation only in a limited way so as not to admit too much optimism: "If this existence is a kind of false step or wrong path, if it is the work of an originally blind will, the luckiest development of which is that it comes to itself in order to abolish itself, then the act perpetuating that existence must appear precisely as it does" (*W*, II, 570).

The Denial of the Will

This Chapter 48 of Volume II that discusses the doctrine of the denial of the will-to-live, is a rather large supplement to section 68 of Volume I. The ideas expressed in section 68 are expanded upon here. Schopenhauer makes another attempt here to explain why human birth and human existence cannot and should not be presupposed to be desirable outcomes. He attempts once again to bring home the viewpoint that human birth should neither be deemed to originate out of nothing, nor be called a chance event, nor an innocent occurrence free of sin and guilt. This is a matter which is very difficult to present to a typical western, rational mind. Nevertheless, Schopenhauer tries his best. Furthermore, in this chapter, more arguments and citations are given to defend the thesis that there is much in common between the essential spirit of New Testament Christianity, as distinguished from Old Testament and Protestant Christianity, and that of the twin eastern faiths of Hinduism and Buddhism. At the same time, this chapter offers more examples of the glorious asceticism of the world-renouncing mystics as well as some interesting gallows-sermons of the last-minute converts to asceticism.

Despite his wide study of the eastern texts, Schopenhauer's reading of the Hindu and Buddhist notion of the undesirability of *samsara*, remains too literal, simplistic and pessimistic. These eastern faiths invoke the myth of reincarnation as well as the ultimate goal of liberation (*moksha/nirvana*) to bring home the message that too much attachment with *samsara* demeans human life. Logical with a cultivated thoughtful life of detachment (not to be misunderstood as total detachment) is a desire not to seek undue perpetuation of *samsara*. Not to seek rebirth into *samsara* for oneself is entirely consistent with a contemplative lifestyle of detachment from excessive worldliness. Hence the spirit of Christianity, as peculiarly expressed by Schopenhauer's favourite poet Calderon, as "man's greatest offence is that he was born" can hardly be deemed comparable to the eastern faiths. Hinduism and Buddhism would rather exclaim: "man's greatest offence is not living a life that will prevent rebirth."

Schopenhauer begins this chapter by pointing out that existence itself is guilt laden, sinful and subject to suffering aside from one's actions performed, virtuous or otherwise: "The ancients, particularly the stoics and also the peripatetics and academics, laboured in vain to prove that virtue is enough to make life happy; experience loudly cries out against this" (*W*, II, 603). The Christian notion of sin is something that parallels the Hindu and Buddhist theory of *karma*, according to Schopenhauer, because both oblige the individual to a fundamental remedy of the problem of existence as such, and not just remain caught up in the goodness and badness of isolated actions:

> St. Paul, Augustine, and Luther teach, works cannot justify, since we are and remain essentially sinners ...
> The innermost kernel and spirit of Christianity is identical with that of Brahmanism and Buddhism; they all teach a heavy guilt of the human race through its existence itself. [*W*, II, 603–604]

If the quality of the actions of one's current life were sufficient to make this existence pain-free and happy, then salvation would be either trivial or redundant:

> If we acted as we ought to act, we should also necessarily be what we ought to be. But then we should not need any "salvation" from our present condition, and such salvation is represented as the highest goal, not only by Christianity but also by Brahmanism and Buddhism, in other words, we should not need to become something quite different from, indeed the very opposite of what we are. [*W*, II, 604]

The radical otherness, the loftiness and the ultimacy and the necessity of salvation as the human goal, makes it elusive, indefinable and larger than the life that we know. Yet it looms before us as the most outstanding feature of our humanity. The possibility of salvation makes human existence the highest of all existences. This is why Hinduism makes *moksha* achievable at the end of several life times. On the basis of cumulative good *karma* of all these existences, the knowledge of *brahman* and being of *brahman* becomes one. The indefinable *nirvana* of the Buddhists is utterly other than *samsara*, although creatively described as sharing a boundary with *samsara* by the second-century philosopher Nagarjuna, similarly requires merit acquired over several life-spans. Impressed with the eastern notions of final emancipation, Schopenhauer painfully labors in his writings to explain that salvation is a remedy for the evil of existence, not just a dose of happiness; it is a lofty task ranging over many lifetimes – one life is bound to fall short of the enormity of the blessed realization. He tries to explain that existence that we find ourselves in (inherited from past *karma*) cannot be viewed as a clean slate. It is already pregnant with suffering, lust, facility and inherent subjection to the will-to-live. The wrong that we do is simply the additional evil to be deposited to the baggage of existence:

> Since we are what we ought not to be, we also necessarily do what we ought not to do. We therefore need a complete transformation of our nature and disposition, that is, the new spiritual birth, regeneration, as a result of which salvation appears. Although the guilt lies in conduct, in the *operari*, yet the root of the guilt lies in our *essentia et existential*. [*W*, II, 604]

The guilt and the consequent suffering of human existence is not merely a by-product of one's deeds, but also has to do with the essential nature of existence as such. Being subject to the eternal justice, being an unwarranted event, less preferable than non-existence, and being heir to inevitable suffering, existence as such is no cause for celebration and glory. Existence is in need of complete transformation and salvation; it can be, rarely but possibly, rescued from its delusion:

> Now if we consider the will-to-live as a whole and objectively, we have to think of it … as involved in a "delusion". To return from this, and hence to deny its whole present endeavour, is what religions describe as self-denial or self-renunciation, "denial of one's own self" (*abnegatio sui ipsius*), for the real self is the will-to-live. [*W*, II, 606]

Schopenhauer continues to describe the steps necessary for the removal of "delusion" (*maya*) and for accumulating merit toward salvation in extreme terms. There seems to be no middle-way, no moderate way, no method of love (*bhakti*) in the "asceticism" he prescribes for the denial of the will-to-live. He does mention in passing that Buddhism is free from excessive asceticism, "that plays a large part in Brahmanism." In fact, Brahmanism too for the most part does not advocate extreme asceticism. The *bhakti* movements within Hinduism showed a method of love for the divine as an alternative to asceticism. Nevertheless, Schopenhauer is much impressed with austere feats and puritanical lifestyles of the *yogis*, *sadhus* and *samanas*:

> Now since … poverty, privations, and special sufferings of many kinds are produced by the most complete exercise of moral virtues, "asceticism" in the narrowest sense, the giving up of all property, the deliberate search for the unpleasant and repulsive, self-torture, fasting, the hair garment, mortification of the flesh; all these are rejected by many as superfluous, and perhaps rightly so. Justice itself is the hairy garment [hairshirt] that causes its owner constant hardship, and philanthropy that gives away what is necessary provides us with constant fasting. For this reason Buddhism is free from that strict and excessive asceticism that plays a large part in Brahmanism, and thus from deliberate self-mortification. It rests content with the celibacy, voluntary poverty, humility, and obedience of the monks, with abstinence from animal food, as well as from all worldliness. [*W*, II, 607]

Thus Schopenhauer remains silent on the moderate path within Hinduism, and does not let the middle way of Buddhism temper his pessimism and the glorification of asceticism. It is interesting that he mentions the "hairy garment," which is indicative of his earnest studies of Vedic and Buddhist texts. Vedas and the Buddhist *sutras* (discourses) refer to the ascetics who donned the hairshirt, even in the scorching summers of India.

In this chapter, Schopenhauer continues to paraphrase the Buddhist concept of *nirvana*, as far as possible, in western terms, and continues to extol the merit of death-contemplation or denial of the will-to-live:

In the hour of death, the decision is made whether man falls back into the womb of nature, or else no longer belongs to her, but_____: we lack image, concept and word for this opposite … However, the death of the individual is in each case the unweariedly repeated question of nature to the will-to-live: "Have you had enough? Do you wish to escape from me?" …

However, he will be least afraid of becoming nothing in death who has recognized that he is already nothing now, and who consequently no longer takes any interest in his individual phenomenon, since in him knowledge has, so to speak, burnt up and consumed the will. [*W*, II, 609]

In a juxtaposition of Vedanta and Buddhism, Schopenhauer outlines his notion of moral action *vis-à-vis* the denial of the will-to-live. Although *samsara* is a term common to Vedanta and Buddhism, "identity of the inner nature of all living things" is clearly a fundamental Vedantic conviction:

The holiness attaching to every purely moral action rests on the fact that ultimately such action springs from the immediate knowledge of the numerical identity of the inner nature of all living things. But this identity is really present only in the state of the denial of the will (*nirvana*), as the affirmation of the will (*samsara*) has for its form the phenomenal appearance of this in plurality and multiplicity … The virtuous action is a momentary passing through the point, the permanent return to which is the denial of the will-to-live. [*W*, II, 609, 610]

In this supplement to Book IV of *WWR*, Schopenhauer again expresses amazement at the fact that quietists, mystics, ascetics, *sadhus*, *samanas* and *sufis* from all parts of the world have all shared one thing in common, namely the denial of the will-to-live. He realizes that his curious combination of philosophy and religious asceticism will not be well received in academic circles, but he finds in this universal practice of asceticism by the holiest and purest world-renouncers, a revalidation of his own philosophy:

If in the judgement of contemporaries, the paradoxical and unexampled agreement of my philosophy with quietism and asceticism appears as an obvious stumbling block, yet I, on the other hand, see in this very agreement a proof of its sole accuracy and truth, and also a ground for explaining why it has been discreetly ignored and kept secret by "protestant" universities.

> For not only the religions of the east, but also true Christianity has throughout this
> fundamental ascetic character that my philosophy explains as denial of the will-to-live.
> [*W*, II, 615]

The remainder of the chapter is devoted to a study of the ancient scriptures and the
works of Christian thinkers, on the issue of celibacy and marriage to prove that in
genuine Christianity marriage was a mere concession for begetting children, but
total abstinence was deemed a true virtue: "In Catholicism the observance of a
perpetual chastity for god's sake, appears in itself as the highest merit of man" (*W*,
II, 619). Schopenhauer reaffirms his conviction that the spirit of old and genuine
Christianity is similar to that of Hinduism and Buddhism, in terms of the world-
denying tendencies and the longing for salvation in these faiths. But "by eliminating
asceticism and its control point the meritorious nature of celibacy, Protestantism
has already given up the innermost kernel of Christianity" (*W*, II, 625). The ascetic
and enchratite spirit of Christianity continues to resurface in cults and sects like
that of the Shakers, Rappists, Raskolnikis, Gichtelians and Trappists, who practice
asceticism, chastity and benevolence.

Toward the end of the chapter, Schopenhauer cites some instances of "bringing
about the denial of the will by one's own deeply felt suffering." The story of Abbé de
Rance, who stumbled upon the severed head of his beloved Madame de Montbazon
after her sudden death, and who reformed the Trappist Order is briefly given. The
chapter ends with some "gallows-sermons" culled from Schopenhauer's favourite
English newspapers like *The Times* and *Galignani's Messenger*. The last words of
the convicts on death row are occasionally profound summations of human existence
and the need for salvation, and are instances of the deepest suffering yielding
profound wisdom. Here is the gallows-sermon by Hocker the convicted murderer
of Delarue as reported in *The Times* dated April 29, 1845 and cited in the chapter by
Schopenhauer: "I am persuaded that unless the natural heart be broken, and renewed
by divine mercy, however noble and amiable it may be deemed by the world, it can
never think of eternity without inwardly shuddering" (*W*, II, 632).

Vanity, Suffering and Life

Chapter 46 of Volume II is a supplement to sections 56–9 of Volume I of *WWR* and
is entitled "On the Vanity and Suffering of Life." This piece offers additional insights
on the favourite theme of Schopenhauer, namely, suffering, which continues to be
treated formally in all phases of his work and informally on every other page of his
writings. In *Parerga* and *Paralipomena*, he will have more to say on suffering in
Chapters 11 and 12.

It would be an error to dismiss Schopenhauer's thoughts on suffering as
the "ravings of a pessimist." To an open-minded reader his work on this issue is
exceptionally brilliant, thoughtful and supported by incontestable facts and solid
arguments, even though the author's conclusions may seem to be rather extreme.
His treatment of the sanctifying nature of suffering is of particular importance to

comprehend his philosophical stance on death and death-contemplation. Elusive happiness, and omnipresent and unfailing suffering, within existence is one of the fundamental reasons for our amazement and wonder at life, the world and the possibility of salvation. Schopenhauer begins with a gloomy picture of life:

> Life presents itself as a continual deception, in small matters as well as in great. If it has promised it does not keep its word, unless to show how little desirable the desired object was; hence we are deluded now by hope, now by what was hoped for. If it has given it, it did so in order to take … All good things are empty and fleeting … the world on all sides is bankrupt and life is a business that does not cover its costs; so that our will may turn away from it. [*W*, II, 573, 574]

The reality of old age and death is often taken as an inevitable sorrow. However, the certainty of death in one stroke inspires a reflective mind to will and live a higher life. Schopenhauer expressed it beautifully:

> Thus old age and death, to which every life necessarily hurries, are a sentence of condemnation on the will-to-live which comes from the hands of nature herself. It states that this will is a striving that is bound to frustrate itself. "What you have willed" it says "ends thus: will something better". [*W*, II, 574]

Sorrow is felt more acutely than well-being and is seldom absent from life. Life is never free from the pangs of the undesirable. Regarding the feeling of pain, Schopenhauer is graphic as well as accurate:

> Only pain and want can be felt positively; and therefore they proclaim themselves; well-being on the contrary, is merely negative. Therefore we do not become conscious of the three greatest blessings of life as such namely health, youth and freedom, as long as we possess them, but only after we have lost them. [*W*, II, 575]

The evils of our world come in various radical but explicit forms. Man's cruel exploitation of fellow human beings, and the rule of war-mongering, fanatical, nationalistic leaders, receives powerful lament and condemnation from Schopenhauer:

> The chief source of the most serious evils affecting man is man himself; man is wolf for man (*homo homini lupus*) …
>
>   For this purpose … an archfiend is more fitted than the rest, and appears in the form of a conqueror; he sets several hundred thousand men facing one another, and exclaims to them: "to suffer and die is your destiny; now shoot one another with musket and cannon" and they do so. [*W*, II, 578]

Slavery and child labour, which were rampant in Schopenhauer's own times, in America and Europe, are similarly deplored and cited as examples of human cruelty. The never-ending poverty and the apathy of the rich have become ongoing evils of our world, and are as true in our day as in Schopenhauer's:

How man deals with man is seen, for example, in Negro slavery, the ultimate object of which is sugar and coffee. However, we need not go so far; to enter at the age of five a cotton-spinning or other factory, and from then on to sit there, every day first ten, then twelve, and finally fourteen hours, and perform the same mechanical work, is to purchase dearly the pleasure of drawing breath. [*W*, II, 578]

Powerful as are the weapons of understanding and reason possessed by the human race, nine-tenths of mankind live in constant conflict with want, always balancing themselves with difficulty and effort on the brink of destruction. [*W*, II, 584]

Of course the authentic acceptance of death gives momentum to contemplative life and weans one away from the inducements of thoughtless worldliness. Nevertheless, death continues to be regarded as the most terrible thing that there is by the innocent. Schopenhauer uses the terror of death as an argument for the undesirable status of life. Schopenhauer is at his pessimistic best in the following passage:

If life in itself were a precious blessing, and decidedly preferable to non-existence, the exist from it would not need to be guarded by such fearful watchmen as death and its terrors. But who would go on living life as it is, if death were less terrible? And who could bear even the mere thought of death if life were a pleasure? ... We console ourselves with death in regard to sufferings of life, and with sufferings of life in regard to death. [*W*, II, 578]

But the most thoughtful passage in the chapter is the following, where Schopenhauer points out that to wonder about the being and the nature of the world is the business of all genuine philosophizing; the enigma of the worldconcept being one of the fundamental problems of philosophy. However, Schopenhauer uses the existence of this problem, to draw his own pessimistic conclusion with a simplistic statement that this world is something that "ought not to be." To state this problem in the eastern terminology, Schopenhauer seems to muddle up the desired life of detachment from *samsara*, the end of *samsara* for oneself (*nirvana*) with abolition of *samsara* as such. But man's philosophical wonder concerning his "world" is thoughtfully outlined by Schopenhauer:

If the world were not something that "practically" expressed ought not to be, it would not be "theoretically" a problem. On the contrary its existence would either require no explanation at all, since it would be entirely self-evident that astonishment at it and enquiry about it could not arise in any mind; or its purpose would present itself unmistakably. But instead of this it is indeed an insoluble problem, since even the most perfect philosophy will always contain an unexplained element ... Therefore if anyone ventures to raise the question why there is not nothing at all rather than this world, then the world cannot be justified from itself; no ground, no final cause of its existence can be found in itself. [*W*, II, 579]

Salvation

"The Road to Salvation" constitutes Chapter 49 of Volume II of *WWR*. Schopenhauer continues to assert that happiness is not the purpose of existence; "The world and life are certainly not arranged for the purpose of containing a happy existence" (*W*, II, 634). Joys and pleasures are often deceptive whereas pains and sorrow "prove very real, and often exceed all expectations." Schopenhauer emphasizes the redemptive quality of sorrow: "The more one suffers, sooner is the true end of life attained, and … more happily one lives, the more is that end postponed" (*W*, II, 635). Turning away of the will from life or denial of the will-to-live is called the true end of life: "In fact, suffering is the process of purification by which alone man is in most cases sanctified, in other words, led back from the path of error of the will-to-live" (*W*, II, 636). Thus suffering is called a purificatory, sanctifying force which brings thoughtfulness and motivation to alter the erroneous submission to the will-to-live. To recognize and accept suffering brings home the insight that happiness is the exception rather than the rule and that the pursuit of happiness without meeting the real challenges of suffering is bound to produce a thoughtless and vulgar life. The purification brought about by suffering also belongs to death, says Schopenhauer: "If suffering has such a sanctifying force, this will belong in an even higher degree to death, which is more feared than any suffering" (*W*, II, 636).

Schopenhauer also remarks on the significance of death as suffering, as it is commonly feared more than anything else. There is a sense of awe in the presence of a dead person; "The guard gets under arms in the presence of every corpse." In the short story "The Death of Ivan Ilych" by Tolstoy, the somber moments of the showing of the body are described quite graphically:

> The dead man lay, as dead men always lie, in a specially heavy way, his rigid limbs sunk in the soft cushions of the coffin, with the head forever bowed on the pillow …
>
> As is always the case with the dead his face was handsomer and above all more dignified than when he was alive. The expression on the face said that what was necessary had been accomplished, and accomplished rightly. Besides this there was in that expression a reproach and a warning to the living.[4]

Death as the summation of life's constant reminders, is described in yet another novel way by Schopenhauer:

> Dying is certainly to be regarded as the real aim of life; at the moment of dying, everything is decided which through the whole course of life was prepared and introduced. Death is the result, the "resume" of life, or the total sum expressing at one stroke all the instruction given by life in detail and piecemeal, namely, that the whole striving, the phenomenon of which is life was a vain, fruitless, and self-contradictory effort, to have returned from which is a deliverance. [*W*, II, 637]

---

4   Leo Tolstoy, "The Death of Ivan Ilych," in *The Death of Ivan Ilych and Other Stories*, A Maude (trans.) (New York: New American Library, 1960), p. 98.

The presence of death in life, death as the final destiny of life, an infallible failure of the advances of life, certainly brings home the truth that pursuit of life's goods, and promotion of life as such cannot be undisputed goals of wisdom. Even though one may not arrive at Schopenhauer's pessimistic conclusion that life is "a vain, fruitless and self-contradictory effort," nevertheless the presence of death obliges one to dispute a thoughtless glorification of life and the forces of life. Death makes life questionable and less worthy of blind worship. For the real sorrows crowned by death indicate that something other than life is equally real and that death is intertwined with life. There is no pure life, just as there is no pure happiness.

Regarding salvation *per se*, Schopenhauer has very little new to say in this short chapter. It is implied in the title of this chapter that he wants to call the denial of the will-to-live "the road to salvation." He reiterates that this denial of the will suggests itself to lesser mortals and sinners by their own sufferings, examples of which were given in previous chapters of Volumes I and II, as occasional realization of one's personal suffering and tragedy (Raymond Lull, Abbé de Rance), or conversion of the death row convicts, or simply sanctification and conversion to contemplative life due to the realization of the sufferings of the world deeply felt by oneself. Then there is a "way of knowledge" realized by the select few, the spiritual masters, who are less known than the heroes of history, but nevertheless revered in all cultures for their saintly lives of renunciation:

> All these considerations furnish a fuller explanation of the purification, the turning of the will, the salvation … which are brought about by the sufferings of life, and are undoubtedly the most frequent; for they are the way of sinners, as we all are. The other way, leading to just the same goal by means of mere knowledge, and accordingly the appropriation of the sufferings of a whole world, is the narrow path of the elect, of the saints, and consequently is to be regarded as a rare exception. Therefore, without that first path, it would be impossible for the majority to hope for any salvation. [*W*, II, 638]

Chapter 6

Schopenhauer:
The Later Essays

After the appearance of the first edition of *The World as Will and Representation* (*WWR*), Schopenhauer published three major works, namely, *On the Will in Nature* (*Der Wille in der Natur*, 1836), *On the Basis of Morality* (*Die Beiden Grundprobleme der Ethik*, 1841) and *Parerga and Paralipomena* (*PP*) (1851). The latter work is the only one in which the issue of death and contemplation is given explicit and protracted treatment. In this work, containing short philosophical essays on various subjects, Schopenhauer compiled the results of almost three decades of reflections, notes and drafts through an editing and writing process that lasted six years. It is this book that won Schopenhauer his well-deserved status as a major thinker and its popular success turned him into a celebrity. The whole of Volume I (*Parerga*) and Chapters 15–31 of Volume II (*Paralipomena*) require no rigorous knowledge of Schopenhauer's previously published philosophical works. The entire work is written in a style even simpler than Schopenhauer's usual clear and concise prose but continues to give evidence of the author's superior knowledge of the western classics, as well as of the newly available eastern sources. In the following reappraisal of Schopenhauer's final thoughts on the subject of death-contemplation and the contemplative life, we will focus on some relevant chapters of *PP*. The following accounts aim at completing the picture of Schopenhauer's works on death and contemplation, and the essays selected do present the results of this thinker's reflections developed in his last phase. In his advanced years Schopenhauer did his writing steadily, showing the fruits of his vast reading of classical and contemporary philosophical texts. In this phase, he retained his interest in, and regard for, eastern thought. In the following appraisals of his final works on death and contemplation, we will particularly reveal his eastern connections and his penetrating insights on Vedanta and Buddhism. We do so without underestimating or denying Schopenhauer's western sources, including his vast knowledge of western classics. We emphasize comparative appraisals of this philosopher's work with Indian thought due to the fact that such treatments are hitherto neglected or only scantily addressed in the current secondary literature on Schopenhauer. Besides these comparative reflections, our chief aim continues to be the revelation of Schopenhauer's comprehensive treatment of the pivotal issue of death and contemplation within the entire body of his published works.

The Indestructibility of Our True Nature

Chapter 10 of Volume II of *Parerga and Paralipomena* contains Schopenhauer's last published treatment of the theme of death. This essay, entitled "On the Doctrine of the Indestructibility of Our True Nature by Death," offers an explicit reassessment of the meaning and aftermath of death, whereas several other essays in *PP* also contain several insights and analyses of human mortality. The purpose of yet another treatment of this subject-matter subsequent to the comprehensive essay "On Death and its Relation to the Indestructibility of Our Inner Nature," included in Volume II of *WWR*, is stated as follows by Schopenhauer at the outset of this final essay on death in *PP*. We will call this and subsequent chapters "essays" even though they are divided into numbered sections and even though Schopenhauer calls this piece a "short selection of isolated observations": "Although I have dealt with this subject consistently and fully in my chief work, I still think that a further short selection of isolated observations will always throw some light on that discussion and will not be without value to many a reader" (*PP*, II, 267).

The theme of death has been "consistently and fully," that is, comprehensively treated, in *WWR* as this pivotal issue ought to be encountered by any genuine philosophy or metaphysics claiming to embrace the nature of things on the whole. This issue pervades the very central concepts of Schopenhauer's philosophy, namely the will-to-live and the possibility of the denial of the will-to-live. Thus this crucial theme of philosophy has been discussed both implicitly and explicitly throughout Schopenhauer's chief work. However, this enigmatic issue can still be enriched by a "further short selection of isolated observations" in his major later work *PP*, says Schopenhauer, which he hopes will prove to be valuable for many readers puzzled by the mystery and implications of human mortality.

The first "false conception" that Schopenhauer wishes to dispel is the wishful thoughts concerning the persistence of one's personal consciousness after death:

> For the true knowledge based on the contrast between phenomenon and thing-in-itself, of the indestructibility of our real nature – a nature that is untouched by time, causality and change – is rendered impossible by the false contrast between body and soul as also by raising the whole personality to a thing-in-itself that is said to last forever. [*PP*, II, 267]

It is not just the wishful thinking that conceives the permanence of the individual personality, but also the false dichotomy between body and soul, so embedded in western metaphysics, that gives rise to this false conception, says Schopenhauer. As he has shown in previous writings, the true nature of the human being perpetuates in another fundamental form and is not destroyed by death. He has also shown that the traditional notion of the soul as the seat of consciousness and intellect is not the primordial being of the human entity. It is the intellect that subserves the will and not vice-versa, the primordial will embodies the body and mind. Thus to raise one's personality or personal consciousness to the level of a thing-in-itself by alluding to notions such as the permanence of the soul does not sit well with Schopenhauer's metaphysics of the will. That he deems personal immortality in the sense of perpetuation of the personality false and absurd is obvious in this final assessment of death in *PP*.

What Schopenhauer presents here is an amalgamation of Vedantic and Buddhist standpoints on death and reality which have been pressed into the service of his own brand of death-contemplation, which is a central theme of his metaphysics of the will. At the same time, in *PP* he presents his positions in simple and pithy writing, for this work was also meant for readers unfamiliar with *WWR*. However, at times "thought" suffers over-simplification at the hands of both metaphysical clarity as well as the beauty of a prose style rigorously pursued by Schopenhauer in his work on the whole. No wonder then that he comes to be a popular philosopher at long last with the publication of *PP* and wins the approbation of non-academic readership in the last decade of his life: "'After your death, you will be what you were before your birth' ... It implies the absurdity of the demand that the kind of existence, which has a beginning ought to be without end; but in addition it contains the hint that there may be two kinds of existence and accordingly two kinds of nothing" (*PP*, II, 268).

In this piece of work, Schopenhauer repeats his earlier assertions in Volume II of *WWR* that we must take into account the ontological status of the human entity before its birth, and not just continue to speculate on what happens after death. Whether we were created out of nothing is a crucial issue. Schopenhauer prefers the Hindu and the Buddhist standpoint, including their myths of reincarnation and rebirth rather than the basic Christian position that man is created out of nothing by a creator God. Although when all is said and done, Schopenhauer prefers the "esoteric" Buddhist theory of *palingenesis* over the popular Hindu and "exoteric" Buddhist belief in metempsychosis, he never abandons the fundamental Vedic insight that all entities are rooted in and pervaded by the Being of beings which Vedanta calls *brahman* and Schopenhauer calls the "will-to-live."

It is the obsession with individual existence that makes one long for its continuation beyond death. It also makes one be oblivious of another trans-personal existence that one has, that can possibly open one's eyes to a universal being, a kinship with all that is. Thus nothing of the loss of one's personal being may not mean nothing at all. Whereas in the essay on death in Volume II of *WWR*, Schopenhauer focused on the continuation of the life of the species vs. the death of the individual to explain "the indestructibility of our true nature," here in *PP* he seems to posit the same by emphasizing one's indestructible universal being vs. the personal being subject to death. This emphasis may have developed due to his deeper studies and appreciation of the Vedanta world-view. Indeed, this deep-seated influence of Vedanta is clearly present in the last passage of this *PP* essay and in the footnote appended to it:

For this is the world of finiteness, suffering and death. What is in it and comes out of it must end and die. But what is not out of it and will not be out of it, pierces through it, all powerful like a flash of lightning which strikes upwards and then knows neither time nor death. To reconcile all these antitheses is really the theme of philosophy. Footnote: ... when a man dies, he should cast off his individuality like an old garment and rejoice at the new and better one which he will now assume in exchange for it, after receiving instruction ... . [*PP*, V, 278]

It is the non-*samsaric* aspect of our existence that remains covered up in our matter-of-course worldly life. But it is our non-*samsaric* being that "knows neither time nor death," which is not destroyed by death. The following passages of the *Bhagvadgita* seems to be the inspiration for what Schopenhauer says in the above quoted lines of the footnote: "It [*atman*] is never born, nor does it die at any time, nor having once come to be does it again cease to be. It is unborn, eternal, permanent and primeval. It is not slain when the body is slain" (II-20); "Just as a person casts off worn outer garments and puts on others that are new, even so does the embodied *atman* cast-off worn out bodies and take others that are new" (II-22).

Schopenhauer has employed the simile in the above quoted passage 22 of the *Bhagvadgita* to reinterpret the insight of passage 20, that the common obsession with individual existence must be overcome to open one's eyes to one's universal being which is deathless. To one who knows this and is well rehearsed in de-emphasizing individual and worldly life, the actual death of his body is a non-threatening non-radical event. Schopenhauer mentions here that to reconcile what is subject to death with what is deathless is really "the theme" of philosophy. This is what Socrates stated through his deed of philosophical martyrdom. The two aspects of our Being, the individual and the universal are stated in the simple and secular terms in this essay. Yet, a deep appreciation of Vedanta is visible in passages such as the following: "No individual is calculated to last for ever; it is swallowed up in death; yet in this way we lose nothing, for underlying the individual existence is one quite different whose manifestation it is. This other existence knows no time and so neither duration nor extinction" (*PP*, II, 269).

Creation out of nothing is an idea that is both unreal and psychologically unacceptable for Schopenhauer: "Everyone feels that he is something different from a being whom another once created out of nothing. From this there arises for him the assurance that death may bring to an end to his life but not his existence ... Man is something different from an animated nothing; and so too is an animal" (*PP*, II, 270). This means that it is inconceivable for one to have a gut feeling of having been nothing. If one regards oneself important enough to last beyond the doors of death, one cannot possibly fathom the possibility of having been nothing before birth.

Since we are familiar and accustomed to only our own individual and worldly existence, we tend to cling to it and even long for its continuation beyond death, which we know to be certain. But it is our unfamiliarity and ignorance of our universal being that makes us love and value our personal being immoderately and even irrationally:

> If we had a complete knowledge of our own true nature through and through to its innermost core, we should regard it as ridiculous to demand the immortality of the individual, since this would be equivalent to giving up that true inner nature in exchange for a single one of its innumerable manifestations, or fulgurations. [*PP*, II, 271]

The undesirability of self-love and excessive self-concern, and the dreamlike status of the *maya* existence are the Vedanta insights endorsed by Schopenhauer in this his last piece of writing on death-contemplation: "The more clearly conscious a man is of the frailty, vanity and dreamlike nature of all things, the more clearly aware is he also of the eternity of his own true inner nature" (*PP*, II, 271).

Furthermore, Schopenhauer repeats, in other words, his explanation, given in Volume II of *WWR*, of the everyday resignation and forgetfulness with respect to death. Whereas all human beings know their death to be certain and possible any moment, nevertheless they seem to have a spark of eternity, almost a gut feeling, which amazingly keeps them immersed in their current worldly projects:

> Whenever we may happen to live, we always stand with our consciousness in the center of time, never at its extremities; and from this we might infer that everyone carries within himself the immovable center of the whole infinite time. At bottom it is this that gives him the confidence with which he goes on living without the constant dread of death. [*PP*, II, 271]

At the same time, Schopenhauer's final essay on death traces the connection between death and knowledge. It is knowledge in the sense of an awakening from *maya*, in the sense of *jnana*, the Vedanta concept of knowing and becoming *brahman*:

> In consequence of all this, life may certainly be regarded as a dream and death as an awakening. But then the personality, the individual, belongs to the dreaming and not to the waking consciousness; and so death presents itself to the former as annihilation: yet at all events, from this point of view death is not to be regarded as the transition to a state that to us is entirely new and strange, but rather only as the return to our own original state, of which life was only a brief episode. [*PP*, II, 272]

Although Schopenhauer is here referring to the event and the aftermath of death, it is also implied that thinking about the truth of death or death-contemplation, too is a knowledge in the sense of awakening, a higher knowledge of our rootedness in an eternal Being, an overcoming of our usual matter-of-course dream (*maya*) life. "The return to our own original state" ought to be interpreted in this sense. Otherwise, the above passage will seem to deny the myth of reincarnation altogether, and can be taken as implying that death is an immediate salvation for all mortals. Accordingly, Schopenhauer does not bypass the issue of rebirth but deals with it once again in this final summation: "That in some sense we should survive death is certainly not a greater miracle than that of generation, which we daily see before us. That which dies passes away to the source whence all life comes, its own included" (*PP*, II, 275).

Here Schopenhauer outlines his own concept of rebirth, which downplays the role of personality or individual being. This view approximates more closely, as Schopenhauer clearly admits (*PP*, II, 276), the Buddhist *palingenesis* based on the no-soul doctrine, rather than the Hindu metempsychosis based on the transition of the soul after death. Schopenhauer describes his own position very thoughtfully in strictly secular terms:

> From this point of view, our life might be regarded as a loan received from death; sleep would then be the daily interest on that loan. Death openly proclaims itself as the end of the

individual, but in him there dwells the seed for a new being. Accordingly, of all that dies, nothing dies forever; but also nothing that is born receives an entirely and fundamentally new existence ...

We might very well distinguish between *metempsychosis* as the transition of the entire so-called soul into another body, and *palingenesis* as the disintegration and new formation of the individual, since his will alone persists and assuming the shape of a new being, receives a new intellect. [*PP*, II, 276]

Although the "disintegration and new formation" model of Buddhist *palingenesis* does resemble Schopenhauer's account of rebirth, it is not easy to locate the all-important reality of the will in the Buddhist doctrine. The *skandha* (aggregate) of *svabhava* (pre-dispositions) which approximates the accumulated *karma* (deeds) of the individual is what undergoes transition in rebirth. Schopenhauer's account of the new formation of the will simplifies the issue of why the rebirth happens in accordance with one's deed in terms of the will's self-perpetuation, as well as the rare acts of its denial by human beings. However, Schopenhauer's notion of the denial of the will is somewhat comparable to the Buddhist concept of *nirvana*.

Schopenhauer briefly compares and contrasts his own standpoint on the aftermath of death with some western theories. He points out that there are references to *palingenesis* in the New Testament in the following two passages: "Matthew 19:28 in the sense of 'resurrection of the dead' and Titus 3:5 in the sense of 'conversion of the old man into the new'" (*PP*, II, 277, footnote). Showing a Buddhist disdain for the concept of the soul, regarding Plato and Aristotle he has this to say:

I am in agreement with Plato insofar as he distinguishes in the so-called soul between a mortal and an immortal part. But he is diametrically opposed to me and to truth when after the manner of all philosophers prior to me, he regards the intellect as the immortal part, the will on the contrary, that is, the seat of appetites and passions, as the mortal. We see this in the *Timaeus* ... Aristotle states the same thing. [Footnote follows]. In *De anima* (1.4) right at the beginning, he lets out incidentally his own opinion that the *nous* is the "real soul and immortal", which he supports with false assertions. He says that hating and loving belong not to the soul, but to its organ, the perishable part. [*PP*, II, 277]

A Dialogue Concerning the Hereafter

This "short concluding diversion in the form of a dialogue" seems to be modeled after David Hume's *Dialogues Concerning Natural Religion*, although Schopenhauer's composition is too short and sketchy to merit comparison with Hume's comprehensive treatise. There are only two interlocutors in this brief dialogue. Thrasymachos, the university-educated, religiously inclined, arrogant, demanding, street-smart individual has a tête-à-tête with the deeply philosophical Philalethes, who seems to be Schopenhauer's mouthpiece. Death and its aftermath is the subject of discussion.

The dialogue begins with an inquiry by Thrasymachos concerning what one would be after one's death. "Everything and nothing" responds Philalethes:

You as an individual end at your death; but the individual is not your true and ultimate essence, but rather a mere manifestation thereof ... Your true essence-in-itself does not know either time, beginning, end or the limits of a given individuality and so it cannot be excluded from any individuality, but exists in each and all. Therefore in the first sense, you become nothing through your death; in the second, you are and remain everything. [*PP*, II, 280]

Thrasymachos is not impressed with an immortality combined with a certain loss of individuality through death. He declares that he cares more for the continuation of his individuality. Philalethes tries to explain that love of individuality is nothing unique in a specific individual, but a deep-seated feeling in all entities that have any trace of consciousness. This will-to-live is "essential to everything that exists, indeed is that whereby it exists, and accordingly is satisfied by existence in general to which alone it refers, and not exclusively through any definite individual existence" (*PP*, II, 281). Philalethes explains that craving for existence is only "indirectly" the individual. Directly it stems from the will-to-live in general, which is "one and the same in all":

It follows from this that individuality is no perfection but a limitation, and to be rid of it is, therefore, no loss, but rather a gain. Therefore give up a fear that would seem to you to be childish and utterly ridiculous if you know thoroughly and to its very foundation your own nature, namely as the universal will-to-live, which you are. [*PP*, II, 282]

Thrasymachos responds most unsympathetically, calls Philalethes himself and other philosophers like him not only childish and utterly ridiculous but also foolish. He would no longer waste his time on a conversation of this sort and departs with a "good bye and God help you."

The destruction of the individual combined with the continuation of the species on the part of will-to-live is something he has already exposed in detail in the essay on death in Volume II of *WWR*. The inherent clinging to one's individuality (*maya*) and an overlooking of one's eternity (*brahman*) is the Vedanta insight that he fuses into his thought more and more in the later phase of his writing. To be rid of mine-ness (*mamta*) is an important virtue for a salvation-bound existence, which overcomes the fear of death in a realization of eternity (*brahman*) in this very life. Schopenhauer's thought echoes the basic standpoints of Vedanta within the fold of his metaphysics of the will.

The Vanity of Existence

In Chapter 11, entitled "Additional Remarks on the Vanity of Existence," Schopenhauer supplements and rephrases his viewpoints on the vain character of human life, first expressed in sections 56–9 of Volume I and Chapter 46 of Volume II of *WWR*. The finite nature of the individual within infinite time and space, the transitoriness of the moment at hand, the dependence and relativity of entities, endless wishes and their obstructions, ceaseless striving and continual frustrations, reveal the vanity of human existence. Schopenhauer seems once again to endorse his reading of Buddhism distorted of course with his deep-seated pessimism. At the same time, he re-expresses his classic explanation of our everyday tranquility against the terrible facticity of death, an explanation in which his own position on the permanence and continual re-emergence of the will-to-live, as well as the Vedanta standpoint on the eternity of *brahman* and rebirth of the soul, remain intact: "Perhaps the sight of this ebbing away of our brief span of time would drive us mad, if in the very depths of our being we were not secretly conscious that the inexhaustible spring of eternity belongs to us so that from it we are forever able to renew this period of life" (*PP*, II, 284).

Schopenhauer restates the insights and principles of his philosophy in a much simpler and more candid expressions in these chapters of *PP*. The human predicament of a matter-of-course subjection to the will and meaningless striving, is summed up beautifully in some passages:

> It must be a matter of surprise to us to see how, in the human and animal world, that exceedingly great, varied and restless motion is produced and kept up by two simple tendencies , hunger and the sexual impulse, aided a little perhaps by boredom, and how these are able to give the *primum mobile* to such a complicated machine that sets in motion the many-coloured puppet-show. [*PP*, II, 285]

As soon as needs and wants are temporarily satisfied, humans are beset by boredom. Schopenhauer presents here an analysis of boredom as a philosophically interesting phenomenon: "Thus if life, in the craving for which our very essence and existence exist, had a positive value and in itself a real intrinsic worth, there could not possibly be any boredom. On the contrary, mere existence in itself would necessarily fill our hearts and satisfy us" (*PP*, II, 287).

Schopenhauer draws his radically pessimistic conclusion concerning "the essential wretchedness of our existence" from the fact that when we are not preoccupied in striving for self-established goals or intellectual pursuits, we find ourselves laden with boredom, a bane of the rich, just as poverty is the bane of the poor. While Schopenhauer does offer brilliant arguments and illustrations in support of his thesis that heroically calls the spade a spade, his thought suffers from a metaphysical over-simplification and exaggeration in the name of clarity. Repeatedly he fails to distinguish between the "undesirability of the excessive worldliness", and that of the world as such and the existence as such. His reading of Vedanta and Buddhism, which he uses to reauthenticate his pessimism, suffers from the same over-simplification. While being too much absorbed in *samsara* and having to come back into *samsara* are not deemed worthy of a higher and truly "human" life in Vedanta and Buddhism, these systems by no means regard human existence as such, as wretched. Human birth and human existence are deemed highest and blissful, for only human existence can live the life of *dharma*, accumulate merit (good *karma*) and be worthy of salvation (*moksha*, or *nirvana*). In other words, Vedanta and Buddhism do not contain the kind of pessimism that Schopenhauer openly and unabashedly embraces. However, if we think of the immoderate and unrealistic claims of the so-called optimists, hymnists and glorifiers, their pronouncements are equally exaggerated. Schopenhauer continues to treat philosophically the awesome truth of death and question its very existence:

> If we were something valuable in itself, something that could be unconditioned and absolute, it would not have non-existence as its goal ... The necessity of death can be inferred primarily from the fact that man is a mere phenomenon, not a thing-in-itself and thus not *ontos on*. If he were, he could not perish. But that the thing-in-itself at the root of phenomena of this kind can manifest itself only in them, is a consequence of its nature. [*PP*, II, 288]

After death we will be, in a sense, nothing, but in another sense, we shall remain, as everything remains, part of the ground of everything and perhaps one will reappear as something different but essentially the same. Death, the muse of philosophy, inspires us to think along these lines and reconceive systematically the nature of existence.

Suffering of the World

In Chapter 12 of *PP*, entitled "Additional Remarks on the Doctrine of the Suffering of the World," Schopenhauer once again reflects on his favourite theme. This chapter, like the previous chapter on the Vanity of Existence, refers back to sections 56–9 of Volume I and Chapter 46 of Volume II of *WWR*. What is additional in these "additional remarks" is stated in the very first paragraph: "It is absurd to assume that the infinite pain, which everywhere abounds in the world and springs from want and suffering essential to life, could be purposeless and purely accidental" (*PP*, II, 291).

The essential and undeniable suffering within human life is not purposeless. The obstacles to our insatiable will that constitute suffering overshadow the limited joys and pleasures, and must teach us a lesson concerning the thoughtless subservience of the will. Schopenhauer has already mentioned that the consciousness of, and empathy with, the infinite sufferings of others and at times, the jolt given by one's own massive loss (*WWR*, II, 630) can inspire asceticism leading to the denial of the will-to-live. Thus enhanced susceptibility to pain in the human entity due to its superior endowment of knowledge makes it suffer far more than any animal. But this very endowment of knowledge contains within itself the possibility of will's self-denial. What Schopenhauer also wants to affirm is that it is not just knowledge but a gut feeling of suffering, enhanced by reflection, memory and empathy with the similar (or worse) lot of others that can possibly nudge one toward a life of the denial of the will-to-live. Thus, perhaps endless suffering does have a purpose. It can galvanize in one the possibility of the denial of the will: "Even the susceptibility to pain could reach its highest point only when, by virtue of our faculty of reason and its reflectiveness, there exists the possibility of denying the will. For without that possibility, such susceptibility would have been purposeless cruelty" (*PP*, II, 298).

As well as this insight on the hidden purpose of human suffering, Schopenhauer repeats his earlier assertions pertaining to the vanity and suffering of existence, in some cases, with new arguments and illustrations. The following is one example:

> Just as we do not feel the health of our whole body, but only the small spot where the shoe pinches, so we do not think of all our affairs that are going on perfectly well, but only of some insignificant trifle that annoys us. On this rests the negative nature of well-being and happiness, as opposed to the positive nature of pain, a point that I have often stressed. [*PP*, II, 291]

Concerning the connection between suffering and death, Schopenhauer is very lucid and blunt:

> The measure of pain increases in man much more than that of pleasure and is now in a special way greatly enhanced by the fact that death is actually "known" to him. On the other hand, the animal runs away from death merely instinctively, without really knowing it and thus without really coming face to face with it, as does man who always has before him this prospect. [*PP*, II, 295]

Even though Schopenhauer acknowledges that the capacity of knowledge and the possibility of the denial of the will-to-live makes the human existence a superior one, yet he can scarcely restrain his propensity toward a drastic pessimism and harsh misanthropy:

> We can regard our life as a uselessly disturbing episode in the blissful repose of nothingness. At all events even the man who has fared tolerably well, becomes more clearly aware, the longer he lives, that life on the whole is a disappointment, nay a cheat … The world is just a "hell" and in it human beings are the tortured souls on the one hand, and devils on the other. [*PP*, II, 300]

At the same time, he continues to justify his extreme conclusions by referring to the eastern systems of thought, which certainly do not regard human birth as "a uselessly disturbing episode in blissful repose of nothingness". Even if we oversimplify *nirvana* as "a blissful repose of nothingness," one cannot simply come in and out of *samsara* in the way described by Schopenhauer. The life of *dharma*, that is, one of detachment from *samsara*, is deemed to be very much possible in human existence. It is not something that one must die for. One does not have to die the actual death to free oneself from *samsara* (or what Schopenhauer calls the will). Thus human existence cannot be called a "uselessly disturbing episode," for it does offer the possibility of freedom from will's oppressive wants and lusts and also the possibility of the denial of the will, resulting in salvation. Besides that, as Schopenhauer himself has said, the knowledge of terrible possibility and certainty of death is mollified by the inner realization of our bond with something eternal. Schopenhauer powerfully abbreviates the accounts of the world's genesis in Hinduism, Buddhism, the Greek tradition, Zoroastrianism, Judaism and Christianity, giving everything his own pessimistic slant:

Brahma produced the world through a kind of original sin, but himself remains in it to atone for this until he has redeemed himself from it. This is quite a good idea. In Buddhism the world comes into being in consequence of an inexplicable disturbance ... in the crystal clearness of the blessed and penitentially obtained state of *nirvana* and hence through a kind of fatality ... An excellent idea. To the Greeks the world and the gods were the work of an unfathomable necessity; this is fairly reasonable ... *Ormuzd* lives in conflict with *Ahriman*; this seems not unreasonable. But that a God *Jehovah* creates this world of misery and affliction ... and then applauds himself, this is something intolerable. [*PP*, II, 301]

By translating "life of *samsara* ought not to be" into "human existence ought not to be," Schopenhauer presents another moral lesson in this regard. Since, as genuine Christianity endorses it, this existence is "a guilt, a false step," and since "man is something that really ought not to be," we must forbear each other and regard "troubles, vexations, sufferings, worries and miseries, great and small" as expected and normal. For, "everyone is punished for his existence and indeed each in his own way" (*PP*, II, 303). This thought is elaborated in the following footnote:

The correct standard for judging any man is to remember that he is really a being who should not exist at all, but who is atoning for his existence through many different forms of suffering and through death. What can we expect from such a being? We atone for our birth first by living and secondly by dying. This is also allegorized by *original sin*. [*PP*, II, 303]

That life and death can both be regarded as the sentence pronounced by original sin or *karma*, that life is a penal colony, are certainly extreme judgments. The Buddha's statement that "birth is *dukkha* (suffering)" is taken too literally by Schopenhauer, just as the role of the *karma* is taken too fatalistically. *Samsara* is not to be our ultimate longing; *dharma* and *nirvana*, here and henceforth, must be the goals. This is what the Buddha meant by "birth is dukkha." And bad *karma* as well as inherited *svabhava* (pre-dispositions) can be rectified, corrected and modified by a moral life of *dharma*. Schopenhauer de-emphasizes and overlooks these optimistic doctrines of Buddhism and Hinduism, although he seems to make a recommendation for the life of the denial of the will-to-live.

More on Suicide

Schopenhauer reconsiders the existential, moral and legal status of suicide in Chapter 13 of *PP*. He had already analyzed the issue of suicide *vis-à-vis* the affirmation and denial of the will in section 69 in Volume I of *WWR*. Both these treatments of phenomenon of suicide are equally brief, about five pages each and contain similar ideas. Schopenhauer maintained in *WWR*, section 69, that suicide cannot be compared to an authentic denial of the will-to-live. It is rather a radical response to the affirmation of the will. A person who commits suicide rejects the possibility of a life of voluntary denial but is often aggrieved about the frustrating outcomes of his affirmation. This is the real reason why no philosophical or religious system finds suicide praiseworthy but instead condemns it unanimously. However, instead of identifying the real reason pertaining to the will-to-live, most ethical theories and religious authorities offer "strange and sophistical arguments" to condemn suicide (*W*, I, 399). Whereas in his first account of suicide Schopenhauer focuses on exposing the relation between suicide and the will-to-live, here in *PP* he emphasizes that suicide is well within the rights of an individual. It is neither a crime against the state nor against society. To associate it with mental illness or insanity is also not legitimate.

Schopenhauer uses the issue of suicide to critique both the monotheistic and Judeo-Christian religions as well as the legal systems, especially the British laws that declared suicide a crime: "The reasons against suicide which are advanced by the clergy of the monotheistic, i.e. Jewish, religions and by the philosophers who accommodate themselves to them, are feeble sophisms which can easily be refuted" (*PP*, II, 309).

At the same time, Schopenhauer clearly exaggerates the incidence of suicide within Hinduism. He mistakenly describes some sporadic Hindu practices as cases of religiously undertaken suicide. For the rare instances of laying under the Jagannath chariot, self-sacrifice to crocodiles and the self-immolation of widows, are the horrific acts of zealots. Such acts are by no means sanctioned by Hinduism, nor are they frequent enough to merit their description as "Hindu practices."

Schopenhauer reiterates what he calls "the only valid moral reason against suicide" earlier enunciated in section 69 of *WWR*:

> It lies in the fact that suicide is opposed to the attainment of the highest moral goal since it substitutes for the real salvation from this world of woe and misery one that is merely apparent. But it is still a very long way from this aberration to a crime, such as the Christian clergy would like to stamp it. [*PP*, II, 309]

However, the real spirit of Christianity does oppose suicide for a fundamental reason, remarks Schopenhauer. Whereas Christianity contains the truth that suffering (the cross) is the noble aim of life, suicide clearly opts out of suffering, and therefore does not embrace the noble purpose. Thus, even though antiquity often approved and honored suicide, Christianity opposes it.

Thus, suicide is a hasty retreat from both the sufferings of life and the possibility of salvation. That is, suicide overlooks the possibility of a life of the denial of the will-to-live but instead rashly rejects life itself.

Nevertheless, acts of suicide clearly denounce a vehemently optimistic interpretation of life characteristic of religions, which describe the creation as "all was very good" (Genesis 1:13): "It is the customary and orthodox optimism of these religions which denounces suicide in order not to be denounced by it" (*PP*, II, 310).

Thus in this six-page final summation of suicide in *PP*, Schopenhauer says what is to be said about this poor substitute of the denial of the will-to-live. Suicide does not deserve religious, social and legal denunciation, for it is well within the rights of an individual to end his life if he so wishes. That suicide is often a reaction to the overwhelming and deeply felt sufferings of life is apparent enough. However, from a moral standpoint, suicide is neither a thoughtful nor a heroic act, for it overlooks the higher possibilities of renunciation, contemplation and contemplative life, It rejects salvation as the goal of life.

More on Affirmation and Denial

In Chapter 14 of *PP*, Schopenhauer offers "additional remarks" on the all-important issue of the possibility of the denial of the will within the usual and all-pervasive human subservience to the will. This chapter, entitled "Additional Remarks on the Doctrine of the Affirmation and Denial of the Will-to-live," presents some supplementary observations and citations on one of the central doctrines of Schopenhauer's system. He begins with a clarification that the denial of the will does not mean annihilation but "the mere act of not-willing; that which hitherto willed no longer wills" (*PP*, II, 312). Schopenhauer acknowledges that "not-willing" is an unfamiliar territory and often described as "passing over into nothing."

In section 163 Schopenhauer seems to imply that the denial of the will is an ethical matter: "My ethics is related to all the ethical systems of European philosophy as New Testament to the Old" (*PP*, II, 314). The Old Testament places man under the authority of a law, which however conveys him to salvation. The New Testament, on the other hand, "preaches the kingdom of grace which is attained by faith, love of one's neighbour, and complete denial of oneself; this is the path of salvation from evil and the world" (*PP*, II, 314). This, Schopenhauer claims, is very much comparable to his own salvation-oriented ethics, all the other prior western ethics being bereft of the goal of salvation:

> My ethics, on the other hand, has ground, basis, purpose, and goal; it first demonstrates theoretically the metaphysical ground of justice and loving kindness and then indicates the goal to which these must ultimately lead ... At the same time it frankly and sincerely admits the abominable nature of the world and points to the denial of the will as the path to redemption therefrom. [*PP*, II, 314]

This "abominable nature of the world" that Schopenhauer labors to expose on the basis of the fundamental pre-supposition of his metaphysics, as well as his creative but peculiar and extreme reading of Vedanta and Buddhism and combined with his sensitive observation and deep-seated empathy for the poor and the systemically exploited sections of humanity, is a matter which is much misunderstood and much berated by his critics. Once again in this piece meant for the popular rather than academic readership, Schopenhauer spells out his position on the undesirable status of *samsara*, a necessary outcome of the depravity of the will that causes a rush of desires, to which the worldling remains subjected:

Whoever is capable of thinking somewhat more deeply will soon see that human desires cannot begin to be sinful first at that point where, in their individual tendencies, they accidentally cross one another ... On the contrary, he will see that, if this is so, they must already be sinful and bad according to their true nature and consequently the entire will-to-live itself is detestable. Indeed the misery and horrors whereof the world is full are merely the necessary result of all the characters in which the will-to-live objectifies itself ... Those horrors and misery are therefore, the mere commentary to the affirmation of the will-to-live. That our existence itself implies a guilt is proved by death. [*PP*, II, 315]

The necessary expiation of the sins (bad *karma*) of a previous existence causes rebirth, an occurrence which makes salvation ever more distant, says the myth of reincarnation, subscribed to by both the Vedic and the Buddhist traditions. However, whereas coming into *samsara* is an untoward event, it does not mean that both the human existence and the world as such are "abominable," evil and full of nothing but pain. Human existence is at the same time an arena, where merit for progress toward salvation is earned. It is also a field which delivers good or bad quality of life, the grading of which is not to be measured just by the criteria of happiness, health and well-being but also by those of virtue, morality, benevolence, will-lessness and sainthood. Since Schopenhauer admits at the outset of this chapter that the life of "not-willing" is regarding which "we are incapable of saying or comprehending what it is" (*PP*, II, 312), he at least acknowledges that such a life is possible and actually lived by some rare and noble souls. Schopenhauer's various accounts of lives of the saints, *sadhus*, *sanyasis*, *sufis* and ascetics indicate that it is possible as well as desirable to live the life of denial, a life that knows and seeks detachment from the bondage of the will. However, Schopenhauer's dichotomy between willing and not-willing, almost taken to the extent of being and not-being, is clearly an extreme view which is at the same time, a metaphysics quite alien to the spirit of Buddhism.

Schopenhauer elaborates on his celebration of an ascetic life of the denial of the will. He cites classical sources indicating that sexual unions were held to be permissible only for the sake of procreation. Pythagoreans were even more radical. According to Schopenhauer, they believed that if coitus is no longer desired for its own sake, it makes marriage and procreation redundant, because denial of the will has already taken place. That is, if human birth is desirable because it is the only existence in which the will can know and deny itself, then in the event of the already obtained denial, further procreation of the human race is rendered unnecessary. The disparity between the promise and reality of romantic love and sexual union is expressed cynically, yet powerfully by Schopenhauer.

Sexual desire, especially when distilled into amorous infatuation through fixation on a definite woman, is the quintessence of the whole fraud of this noble world; for it promises so unspeakably, infinitely and excessively much, and performs so contemptibly little (*PP*, II, 316).

Schopenhauer's pessimism is in a way rooted in his realism. That he has an almost Buddha-like sensitivity to the pain of others is obvious to any careful reader of his works. What we often disregard in our religious glorification of human existence and human society is often powerfully lamented by Schopenhauer. The widespread poverty and want, the slave labour, the exploitation of the blacks in North America, the rampant selfishness, pettiness and malice in interpersonal relations are strongly felt and mourned by him: "The number of regular Trappists is naturally small; but yet half of mankind consists of involuntary Trappists; poverty, obedience, absence of all pleasures and even of the most necessary means of relief, and frequently also chastity … are their lot" (*PP*, II, 319).

In this chapter, Schopenhauer recounts various ways and devices by which the denial of the will can be brought about. Of course, a voluntary embracing of asceticism in the light of the knowledge of the machinations and traps of the will's affirmation is the best course. The "next best course" is the right attitude toward suffering and misery both our own and that of others, in a realization of the positive nature of pain: "Whoever through such considerations realizes how necessary to our salvation misery and suffering usually are will see that we should envy others their unhappiness rather than their happiness" (*PP*, II, 320).

Schopenhauer sums up his powerfully expressed and thoughtful but pessimistic fusion of eastern and western world-views on the issue of the nature and destiny of human existence: "A 'happy life' is impossible; the best that man can attain is a 'heroic life', such as is lived by one who struggles against overwhelming odds in some way and some affair that will benefit the whole of mankind, and who in the end triumphs, although he obtains a poor reward or none at all" (*PP*, II, 322).

Epilogue

The connection between death and contemplation is often underestimated. It has been pointed out in western as well as eastern classics that philosophizing as well as the living of a philosophical life is prompted, inspired and set into motion by a recognition of human mortality. The recognition and contemplation of death is not a pursuit of physical death but a renewed and holistic appreciation of existence and a resolute search for meaning of a thoughtful life. To trace the fuller implications of the practice of death within life and of the reason why death-contemplation has been called both an inspiration and the content of the act of philosophizing, we chose the methodology of tracing this issue within the work of a single thinker, whose philosophical thought revolves around the pivotal issue of death. Schopenhauer is claimed here to be a death-contemplator whose philosophical system is conceived in a full recognition and practice of death in the Socratean tradition. He also happens to be a thinker who sought the validation of his philosophical truth in traditions of philosophical thought other than his own, and attempted to make eastern concepts part and parcel of his own philosophical system. It is fascinating to pursue the issue of death and contemplation through the body of work of a thinker who let death inspire his pathway to philosophy in the classical Socratean tradition, and who studied the classics and the history of philosophy seeking the meaning of human life in the shade of death.

When a philosophical problem is pursued through the system of a single thinker, rather than through a series of brief accounts of the works of several philosophical figures in the form of thematic anthologies and comparative assessments, we have some advantages as well as some possible pitfalls. The advantage is that one can interpret the standpoints of a thinker on a certain theme, critically evaluate the interpretations of other scholars and contribute toward a better understanding of his or her work. An even bigger advantage accrues when one thinks alongside the thinker about the problem at hand and the activity of philosophizing finds an impetus in the innocent admiration and appreciation of the seminal work of an original thinker. The disadvantage of this approach is that one may overlook an historical perspective and may get bogged down in the prejudices of the thinker being studied.

Thus we have tried to study the work of Schopenhauer from a single perspective of death-contemplation which we claim to be his central insight, and which penetrates his central concept of the will-to-live. We have tried not to miss the historical perspective and have traced the roots of his pre-suppositions in the classics of both western and eastern traditions. The connection between death and philosophy is lucidly posited in the antiquity of western thought, in the word and deed of Socrates, who did not take his own death as a calamity but rather explained it as a crowning of a life-long practice he underwent as a philosopher. His sacrifice, his philosophical mission and his death-contemplation have been celebrated and emulated over the centuries by a series of authentic philosophers who made the contemplation of death part and parcel of their philosophical enterprises. Plotinus downplayed the matters of the body in his own way and recommended that through the cultivation of death-contemplation one can shut one's eyes and "change to another way of seeing which everyone has but few use."[1] In more recent times, both Schopenhauer and Heidegger show their debt to Socrates in their respective world-views. That death is a central issue in their otherwise distinct thought systems is quite evident in their pivotal concepts. The will-to-live and the denial of will-to-live in the case of Schopenhauer and the notions of Dasein, Dasein's authenticity and the world-concept in terms of the fourfold (*Geviert*) in the case of Heidegger, are indicative of these thinkers' thanatological orientations.

In the eastern tradition, in roughly the same age as that of Socrates, Plato and Aristotle, a classical statement concerning death-contemplation was made quite thoughtfully and symbolically in the *Katha Upanishad*. In this work, young Naciketas travels to the house of death and lets death be his guru. Death, or the god of death, Yama, is shown as a giver of boons to the seekers of philosophical truth like Naciketas. "Another teacher of it, like of thee is not to be obtained. No other boon equal of it is there at all," exclaims Naciketas about the lessons of Death.[2] The young philosopher learns about the great passing-on (*samparaye*) to be practiced by a seeker of truth. This classic text of Vedanta philosophy is remarkably comparable to Plato's *Phaedo*, even as Socrates and Naciketas are shown as practitioners of death in pursuit of philosophy. Vedanta philosophy will be just as influential as that of Plato and Kant in the development of the philosophical system of Schopenhauer.

Schopenhauer's concept of the denial of the will-to-live appears in Book IV of *WWR*. The practice of such denial is explained in quite secular terms, consistent with the thinker's opposition to the intermingling of Judeo-Christian dogmas with philosophy, apparent in his contempt for Hegel's philosophizing. This denial of the will-to-live is Schopenhauer's own version of the downplaying of the matters of the body put forward by Socrates and Plotinus. True philosophy and authentic living in the shade of philosophy, begins with a voluntary denial of the will-to-live, that the worldly life is subjected to as a matter of course. To be able to overcome that subjection is true freedom and the beginning of a contemplative life. By combining the insights of Vedanta and Buddhism with his deep study of the classics and history of western philosophy, Schopenhauer shows the rewards of his own death-contemplation in his own philosophical achievement. His eastern connections have not been exposed adequately in the secondary literature. Often this influence is recognized but downplayed by Schopenhauer's critics due to their own innocence regarding Vedanta and Buddhism.

---

1   Plotinus, 1.6.7–8, p. 127.
2   *Katha Upanishad*, 1–22.

The issue of whether Schopenhauer's reading of Vedanta and Buddhism is fair and well-balanced even for his age when eastern texts were scantily available, is thoroughly examined in our study. We conclude that although his interpretations of Vedanta and Buddhism are coloured by his deep-seated pessimism, his contribution is not to be underestimated. He was the first major thinker to regard the body of world philosophy as one. He practiced a trans-culturalism far ahead of his times. Indian philosophy was a fascinating discovery for him and he embraced it in a remarkably creative way within his system.

Schopenhauer's preoccupation with death-contemplation was a life-long affair, visible in all phases of his writings. In the supplements he added to his *magnum opus* in its later editions, he expanded on his expositions of the denial of the will-to-live. He comments on the lived philosophies of numerous saintly figures, both Christian and non-Christian, to show what such a life of denial is like. We have shown that whereas his system suffers due to a metaphysical subscription to a grand dualism between the will-to-live and its denial, and due to over-simplifications of a neatly designed metaphysical architectonics, it is not without a remarkable array of fascinating existential insights. His exaggerations never cease to be instructive.

Schopenhauer's long-awaited rise to fame with the publication of his popular essays in the volumes of *Parerga and Paralipomena* does not show any abatement of death-contemplation, to which he devotes a number of new essays. He shows the impact of his continuing scholarship of his eastern sources in this last phase of his creative life. The commentaries on the very real nature of human sufferings brought on by human subservience to the will-to-live adorn these final essays by a thinker who refuses to acknowledge any solutions shorter than a denial of this will. Therein lies the salvation of this existence, which according to Schopenhauer is fraught with the pain of an ignorant and ongoing service of the will. Existence does offer us a chance to know the machinations of the will and a possibility to deny it, in thought and in life, "For a happy life is impossible, the best that man can attain is a 'heroic' life."[3] This heroism demands walking on the razor's edge[4] of death-contemplation.

---

3   PP, II, p. 322.
4   *Katha Upanishad*, 3–14.

Bibliography

Armstrong, A.H. (ed. and trans.), *Plotinus* (New York: Collier Books, 1962).

Atwell, John E., *Schopenhauer: The Human Character* (Philadelphia, PA: Temple University Press, 1990).

Burnet, J., *Plato's Phaedo* (Oxford: Oxford University Press, 1972).

Cartwright, David E., "Schopenhauer on Suffering, Death, Guilt and the Consolations of Metaphysics," in Eric von der Luft (ed.), *Schopenhauer: New Essays* (Lewiston, NY: Edwin Mellen Press, 1988).

Choron, J., *Death and Western Thought* (New York: MacMillan Company, 1963).

Demske, James M., *Being, Man and Death: A Key to Heidegger* (Lexington: University Press of Kentucky, 1970).

Fox, Michael (ed.), *Schopenhauer: His Philosophical Achievement* (Sussex: Harvester Press, 1980).

——, "Schopenhauer on Death, Suicide and Self- Renunciation," in M. Fox (ed.), *Schopenhauer: His Philosophical Achievement* (New York: Barnes and Noble Books, 1980).

Gambhirananda, Swami (trans.), *Eight Upanishads: with the Commentary of Sankara* (Calcutta: Advaita Ashrama, 1989).

Hadot, Pierre, *Plotinus or the Simplicity of Vision*, M. Chase (trans.) (Chicago, IL: University of Chicago Press, 1993).

Halbfass, Wilhelm, *India and Europe: An Essay in Understanding* (Albany: State University of New York Press, 1988).

Heidegger, Martin, "Plato's Doctrine of Truth", J. Barlow (trans.), in W. Barret and H.D. Iken (eds), *Philosophy in the Twentieth Century* (New York: Random House, 1962), Vol. III, pp. 251–70.

——, *What is Called Thinking*, J. Glenn Garry (trans.) (New York: Harper and Row, 1968).

- ——, "The Thing,", A. Hofstadter (trans.), in *Poetry, Language, Thought* (New York: Harper & Row, 1971).

Holck, F.J., *Death and Eastern Thought* (New York: Abingdon Press, 1974).

Hume, Robert Ernest (trans.), *The Thirteen Principal Upanishads* (Oxford: Oxford University Press, 1931).

Jowett, B. (trans.), *Phaedo*, in *Dialogues of Plato* (Chicago, IL: Encyclopaedia Britannica, 1950).

Luft, Eric Von der (ed.), *Schopenhauer: New Essays* (Lewiston, NY: Edwin Mellen Press, 1988).

Magee, Bryan, *The Philosophy of Schopenhauer* (New York: Oxford University Press, 1997).

Nanajivako, Bhikku, *Studies in Comparative Philosophy* (Columbo: Lakehouse Publishers, 1983).

Nicholls, Moira, "The Influences of Eastern Thought on Schopenhauer's Doctrine of the Thing-in-itself," in C. Janaway (ed.), *The Cambridge Companion to Schopenhauer* (Cambridge: Cambridge University Press, 1999).

Pieper, J., *Death and Immortality*, Richard Winston and Clara Winston (trans.) (New York: Herder and Herder, 1974)

Radhakishnan, S. (trans.), *The Principal Upanishads* (London: George Allen and Unwin, 1978).

—— and Moore, C., *A Sourcebook in Indian Philosophy* (Princeton, NJ: Princeton University Press, 1973).

Rickman, H.P. (ed.), *W. Dilthey: Selected Writings* (Cambridge: Cambridge University Press, 1976).

Schopenhauer, Arthur, *The World as Will and Representation*, E.F.J. Payne (trans.) (New York: Dover Books, 1969).

——, *Parerga and Paralipomena*, E.F.J. Payne (trans.) (Oxford: Clarendon Press, 1999).

——, *On the Will in Nature*, E.F.J. Payne (trans.) (New York: Berg, 1994).

——, *On the Basis of Morality*, E.F.J. Payne (trans.) (Oxford: Berghahan Books, 1995).

——, *On the Fourfold Root of the Principle of Sufficient Reason*, E.F.J. Payne (trans.) (La Salle, IL: Open Court Press, 1974).

——, *Der Handschriftlicher Nachlass*, Arthur Hübscher (ed.) (Frankfurt am Main: Kramer, 1970).

——, *Gesammelte Briefe*, Arthur Hübscher (ed.) (Bonn: Bovier, 1987).

Schwaab, Raymond, *La Renaissance Orientale* (Paris: Payet, 1950).

Singh, R. Raj, "Death-contemplation and Contemplative Living: Socrates and the Katha Upanishad," *Asian Philosophy*, 4 (1994): 9–16.

——, "Death, Contemplation and Philosophy: Heideggger and the Legacy of Socrates," *De Philosophia*, 6 (1986): 41–61.

——, "The Pivotal Role of Bhakti in Indian World-Views," *Diogenes*, 156 (1991): 65–81.

——, "The Ancient Origins of *Bhakti* and the *Dharma* of the Buddha," *Journal of Dharma*, 22(1997): 460–69.

——, "Bhakti as the Essence and Measure of Art," in G. Marchiano and R. Milani (eds), *Frontiers of Trans-culturality in Contemporary Aesthetics* (Turin: Trauben, 2001).

——, *Bhakti and Philosophy* (Lanham, ML: Rowman and Littlefield, 2006).

Tolstoy, Leo, *The Death of Ivan Ilych and Other Stories*, A. Maude (trans.) (New York: New American Library).

Wolz, Henry G., *Plato and Heidegger* (London: Associated University Presses, 1981).

Zimmern, Helen, *Schopenhauer: His Life and Philosophy* (London: George Allen and Unwin, 1932).

Index